To Lily.

My darling daughter, light of my life.

A piece of me, for you, when you need it most.

410 Terry Ave N, Seattle, WA 981091

First published by KDP in 2024

Gylisa Jayne has asserted her right to be associated with this Work in accordance with the Copyright, Designs and Patent Act 1988

www.kdpamazon.com

A CIP catalogue record of this book is to be made available in the British Library

Cover design by Gylisa Jayne

This book is based on the life, experiences and recollections of the author. In some cases, names of people, places, dates and sequences or small details of events have been changed to protect the privacy of others.

After Laughter

Gylisa Jayne

Chapter Index –

Prologue.

After laughter…

…comes tears…

As I write this, the song tinkles out of the TV speakers as I listen to it for the hundredth time today. It's by Wendy Rene, a sixties soul singer, and the moment I heard it I added it to the Crying Playlist.

Do you have one? I haven't met many people that do, I'm usually met with looks of bewilderment when I mention it, but I'm used to that now. I am a *professional over-sharer.* Most people think I'm joking. Some will nod along, wanting to kindly acknowledge my madness. Others change the subject quickly in case I burst out crying there and then.

But I don't do that anymore.

Then – very occasionally - I strike lucky and find my people. My *crying-cos-it-feels-good people.* The people who feel everything as deeply as I do and have found their own crafty little outlet for all that emotion.

It doesn't really matter which camp you fall into, surely you cannot deny that having a good cry feels fucking great. It cleanses me, like a rainstorm washing away all the dust and dirt of crazy hot summer.

My Crying Playlist is on now because I *need* to write this book.

When I began writing, I quickly realised I didn't really have a choice on what I wrote, it just flies out of my fingers exactly how I think it, all wild and raw and strange and sometimes, *sometimes* I get this urge to write something specific, and I can't write or think about anything else until it's been done.

This is one of those times, so here I am – Crying Playlist on repeat, because I need to cleanse myself of this burden, I need to rid myself of this weight, so it might find whoever might need to read it. That's the joy of writing.

Maybe that person will be you.

Maybe it'll be a friend of yours.

It could be a total stranger, someone who has picked up this book and thinks '*Who's this cunt droning on?*' but starts reading anyway.

They might love it. You might too. Of course, you might also think it's the biggest waste of your free time since they invented the iron and find a way to contact me to personally complain. You are welcome to. I'll print it off and frame it next to my mirror - just to humble myself every morning. I think it's important to stay grounded like that.

Anyway.

This book is about grief.

I know - how depressing. But stay with me, because it's quite important.

Death has happened to so many people around me, not that I'd paid them much notice when it did. I didn't understand the gravity of it I suppose - I always felt too young, too removed, too busy living my own life. It always felt like something extra on the To-Do List, that I'd get round to eventually. Like dusting the skirting boards. I had ages before I'd need to worry about that. This was happening to *them,* not *me* – so I'd shrug it off, and carry on with my life. *Selfish little swine that I am.*

To be honest - quite often I purposely looked away, not wanting the wake-up call that death can bring to us – or worse, I'd peer in at their grief in the same way one gawps at a car crash after being held up for thirty minutes on the M25.

Of course, you don't *really* want to see the smashed, blood-spattered windscreens, or some poor souls body parts strewn across the tarmac. *How ghastly.*

And yet, this tendril of morbid curiosity compels us to look.

Plus – *you'll reason with yourself here* - you've been held up on your journey, so it feels almost like a little treat to see some of the horrors from the safety of your car.

Have a little nose, go on…

This is just one of many small interactions in our day-to-day that lull us into a false sense of security around death and dying. Accidents always happen to someone else; so we peek round nosily to see what horrors lie ahead for someone else to deal with.

For someone out there, it'll be the worst day of their life.

But for you, it's just another Tuesday.

You'll drive past and then get engrossed in the radio, or trying to beat the rainclouds home.

Now though, grief, death and dying *was* happening to me and I'd realised how selfish I'd been.

I wanted to grab the people I'd previously lost to the deep recesses of grief and beg them. 'How? How did you get through all of this?'

I'm drowning here. The current is too strong, the waves are too great.

'How did you learn to function again?'

Save me, even though I didn't try to save you.

The shame of not being there for people I knew had loved and lost, kept me from reaching out, even though I could see them struggling. We've all done it haven't we? Why is that? Why do we avoid the difficult conversation, even when we can see someone needs it? Is it ignorance, selfishness or self-preservation?

It reminds me of something I learned years ago.

If you try to save someone from drowning, the risk of drowning yourself increases tenfold – did you know that?

In the panic and confusion and their survival instincts kicking in, they push and kick, flail and gasp. They'll pull you under just to get their own head above water again.

The perfect drowning victim needs to be still and quiet, ready to accept help.

But drowning happens suddenly, and without warning. You don't get a pamphlet handed to you as the water swallows you whole. All you know is you need air to survive.

If you jump in to save a drowning person, without knowing how to safely do so - it could cost your life.

Do you know how the US marines train to save people from drowning?

They jump in, knock the person out, and drag them back out to safety. Incapacitation is the safest way to get a panicking, scared person to survive.

Grieving feels like drowning. It feels like the heavy suffocating weight of water engulfing you, it feels like you have forgotten how to breathe. It feels like darkness with envelope you and never let you go…

So, knock me out and carry me to safety. I think it now, bitterly. When the danger has passed, then I'll come to. Healed and feeling better. Wrapped in a comfortable towel, with a mug of tea pressed into my hand. *Have this, you're safe now.*

Now, what a cheat code that would be.

I felt far too guilty to admit my mistakes. I didn't want to sidle up to them and beg them for their wisdom now I needed it. I didn't want to admit I'd seen their grief and simply looked the other way. That I had thought their grieving was too sad, too final, too depressing. Too all encompassing, and like dangerous, dark water. I was too busy living, happy and safe in my ignorance.

I had ignored it for so long, I simply didn't know how to ask for help when I needed it.

The truth is, most of us will ignore death until it shows up at our door, knocking for us.

Or worse, for someone we love.

Now, I see that getting comfortable with grief, before it appears for us – can actually soften the blow. It's not as confusing and scary and difficult once we look at it properly.

Although I felt so alone in my grief, truly – I wasn't. This new club I found myself in, specifically – The Dead Dad Club – it was going to recruit everyone I knew.

They could ignore it if they wanted. I know I did. *'Oh, that's centuries away'* I'd tell myself, the same way I'd consider grandchildren or thinking a Time-Share might be a 'healthy investment'.

'I'll be more prepared when he's an old man.'

But Dad didn't get to be an old man. In fact, there are no guarantees that any of us will get to those final hurdles.

And yet.

And yet – we tell ourselves it's a given.

The scariest truth of it all is - unless it's you that goes first, you'll grieve for everyone you've ever known and loved.

So, my warning is this: *Grief **will** come for you.*

Could be in a few months, could be years. But Grief will knock at your door, so you might as well get to know it now, from the safety of your car as you pass my car crash. Have a look, make a face. Wish me well, or recoil backwards. But look, read, understand, try to make sense of it.

You may need it sooner than you think.

Whilst in my darker days, I'd wallowed bitterly in that thought. Fate had been particularly unkind to me, as Dad's birthday is on Father's Day. What an absolute shitter that is. Fate has played me a blinder there, the one day that I would think of him the most, wishing more than anything that I could reach out to him just once more – was the same day everyone else would loudly sing about their very alive, annoyingly perfect fathers. I'd scroll angrily through their posts, darkly thinking *'Yeah, we'll see.'*

Lighter days came, of course. Then I'd look at those posts sadly. How fucking depressing. *You've got so much more to lose than me.*

I knew what was coming for them. Jealousy was replaced with a need to urge people to tell their parents how loved they were. To see them even when it felt inconvenient. Take the photos, sing their praises whilst they are still able to hear them. Ask them questions, learn as much as you can while you can. I wanted to protect anyone from the pain they had coming. Try to ease them into grief before it had begun.

Of course, no one listens.

Then they join the Dead Dad Club and it's my hand there first, leaning over to pull them out the water. To show them how to swim. *Don't panic.* It's ok. It's not, but it will be. *I promise.*

As I came through it, once more reaching to pick the familiar scab of grief to discover only a scar remained – I knew that the warning wasn't enough. I didn't want to toll the bells of gloom at people, I wanted to reassure them – the way a loving hand wordlessly squeezes yours when you are upset.

So perhaps, knowing what I know now - I'd like to change that warning to this:

*Grief will come for you - but you **will** get through it.*

This is my grief - it's complicated and messy, the way relationships can be. Not everything will ring true for you, that's OK. For some, it'll clang so loudly you'll wonder if I've bugged your house, listening in. I haven't, but that's the nature of life. So different and yet so familiar for plenty of us.

Either way, I hope it may help you in the future, or perhaps even in the now. I know I needed to hear this back then, so maybe you will be able to look at the impending wave of grief and feel bolstered.

If I can do it, you can too.

Chapter 1 – Don't Fear the Reaper

The thought of Death has never really *scared* me.

Sure, like most -the thought of going in a fiery - screaming - suitcases to the face- oxygen masks flapping down – *mayday-mayday* - no survivors – plane crash situation is rather horrifying to consider.

Or - imagine slipping over in the shower mid-song, being discovered naked and all pale and bloaty, with the last song playing on your Spotify and everyone discovering that, no – your music taste wasn't as refined as you liked to make out.

'Did you hear what she was listening to when she went?'

'Oooh I know!'

Or perhaps, if my cats are still about and I go down clutching my chest for some unknown and obviously rare hidden disease that has suddenly become active after lying dormant for years, I'll be found half chewed, with no eyelids, only recognisable by my dental records or something equally vile.

I suppose, if we could choose, I guess a quiet slipping off in your sleep is always preferred. A bit boring, and hardly memorable - but overall, a more pleasant end to it all.

I know so many people who are utterly terrified of being 'dead'.

They won't talk about it (I've tried), they don't want to speculate with me on the time or manner, and they won't even look at my spreadsheet of statistics to figure out the most likely cause of death organised by age, health factors and social status. (For most it's cancer, or heart disease. *How woefully boring.*)

I guess not everyone shares my penchant for dreaming up deliciously random and exciting methods of carking it.

I think perhaps it's the prospect of being Gone...

Stop.

The Last Hurrah.

Fin.

The End.

What would it feel like? What would it sound like? (Ear splitting screaming and engines whirring if Scenario One is your unfortunate demise) Will I be alone?

Is there a Heaven? Or a Hell?

Who knows?

The thought of my own mortality is, if anything – I'll pause here, look around, to see if anyone else was listening, eyes aflame with wickedness, lean into your ear and whisper - *quite exciting.*

I've considered it so often over the years that I would wholly say – I have made my peace with it. Death is inevitable. Death is intriguing. It could happen dramatically; it could happen tragically. It could be gentle. Death can be sudden. Death can be slow.

It creeps closer all the time, that is for certain. *How thrilling.*

Now I don't want you to get confused that I wish to be dead. Goodness gracious no, I am far too busy living! And I love living! I'd be quite miffed if it was all cut short far sooner than intended. I have so much more left to do, I don't want to shuffle off this realm with an incomplete To-Do List! That would not do at all!

I think, if anything – my fascination with death has led me to cram as much in as possible, as I have seen death enough times now to realise that it discriminates against no one. It's taken friends from me, a parent, a child, a cousin, a confidant and both grandparents - and thousands in between. Whilst others find that thought depressing and morose, I see it as a bony kick up the arse from Mr Reaper himself.

Get busy living, you don't know how long you have left.

In my short time so far, I've packed plenty in. So, I hope by the end - I get there and think, thank fuck – I could do with a rest now.

With that in mind, let's begin...

I was four years old when I first saw death.

My mum was walking my twin brother Tom and I to the library, or preschool or somewhere, that part isn't really an imperative part of the story.

In the gutter lay a beautiful white cat. My memories of this incident are hazy, given that I was so young, but I remember watching the emotion my mum was clearly holding in, as she gently scooped up this poor animal and carefully lay it under a tree. She displayed such compassion for this strangely still cat as she brushed the grit and mud from the underside, placing it into a curled-up position. We must have been asking her what was going on, as kids do - usually loudly - when you are trying to be discreet.

'What's wrong with the cat Mummy?' 'Why does it look like that Mummy?' 'Why are you moving it there, Mummy?'

She spoke so softly, as she worked, tucking the tail around its feet. *'It's just sleeping'* She assured us. And it looked true. The cat lay tucked underneath the iron fence, beneath the tree, sleeping.

There had been an atmosphere of something 'different' when it happened. We went off and didn't think about it, I'd imagine. But I *remember* it vividly now, the strangeness of it all, knowing something poignant had happened, but not exactly sure what.

Mum did what Mums do of course, protected us from the cruelty of life – some arsehole has run over someone else's beloved pet and screeched off to leave it to die in the gutter. Not a second thought. But to us, it was a pristine creature, forever sleeping soundly under those bushes.

My second early memory of death was when I was eight years old.

A boy at my primary school, Scott - upon whom I happened to have a huge crush on, and therefore kept his every movement under my radar – died suddenly. I had for a short period wondered if I'd killed him with my obsessive thoughts, but it turned out he had a rare brain illness – no one would have spotted it. And then he died. Just like that. We didn't know this at the time, it had seemed like one moment he was running around, and the next he just dropped down dead. Once again, we'd gathered round to have this explained to us, and that familiar feeling of something poignant and sombre taking place drapes over my memory it.

Not long after this, Jess - our family cat, pegged it.

It had been a running joke in our household, as Jess would sleep with all four legs in the air – as if she had fallen off the ceiling mid-step. She had stumpy little legs after jumping out of the first-floor window of my mums flat when she'd first got her as a kitten. She was a barrel of a cat, with these tiny useless legs, so when she was upended it really looked odd. *'The cats dead!'* One of us would call to the others as we walked past her. Until one morning, as I walked through the hall to find my school uniform, and stroked her stiff, cold body. Oh, I'd thought. *That's different.*

'Mum, the cats dead.' I'd said, whilst pressing her harder to make sure.

Mum had laughed back.

'Ha, ha – get your shoes on then…'

'No – really- '

We buried her under the bird table, not that the little fatty had ever caught one. And now she never would. Off to the big cat basket in the sky.

I don't mean to sound heartless about it, I was truly upset. I'd written a poem and read it for her 'funeral' whilst Mum, Dad, my twin brother Tom and my sister Clair all sniggered about it.

I'd also harboured guilt that I'd murdered the cat after discovering either mine or Toms squishy ball had punctured – and we'd hung it on the key pegs – above her water bowl. The silver liquid inside dripping ominously out of it, and straight into her dish. I'd fretted for hours that I was a monster, with two kills under my belt – first Scott, now Jess.

Mum reassured me later that she was just very old, and these things happened when you get old.

Scott wasn't old though; I'd thought to myself in bed that evening. *And he's dead.*

I'm not sure if this was what began my curiosity around death, but I did think about more often than was perhaps normal. At eight years old, the thought of death was sad, yes. But that was when I first noticed a little part of me finding the notion quite exciting. Being dead garnered an awful lot of love and attention. Granted, I hadn't connected the dots that the attention would be pointless given that you'd be, well – dead.

I'd watch 'This Is Your Life' on television with my Grandma and Grandad, and would begin crying silently as in my childlike brain I had been so sucked in by this celebrity's loved ones telling them how great they are, I was sad that they'd now be off to die. It took longer than I wish to admit for me to realise they didn't murder the celebrity in the green room after. 'Right, you've had a good run – now into the fucking incinerator you go!'

Where some little girls spent their time crafting their vision of their wedding, I was more preoccupied with the idea of planning my own funeral. This stayed with me as I got older, and I still do it now – if someone irritates me, they are immediately, silently, uninvited from my funeral.

Of course, sometimes, I will reinvite them – just so they can hear all the lovely and wonderful things people would say in my eulogy and feel dreadful about what ever slight they had done to me whilst I was still here. I cackle wickedly at the thought.

When my Grandad died, death was slow. He had cancer, and although they could afford private healthcare, Grandad decided he'd done enough of life and was simply in Gods Waiting Room now. He may as well leave Grandma to the life she'd become accustomed to and spent the last few weeks having his own living funeral.

The last time we spoke to him was very awkward and clunky. I loved my Grandad, of course – but my sister, Clair had always been his favourite.

He used to call her his 'teenage dream' which in a post-Savile era doesn't quite have the same sweet ring to it. My Grandad wasn't a paedophile though, I just want to say that. He was a very lovely old man. It's quite bizarre to say goodbye to someone who you know is about to cark it. There's an element of wondering if they are waiting to hear what you have to say before yelling 'Sike! I knew you loved me!' and springing out of the bed like Charlie Buckets benefit-scrounging grandpa, off to the chocolate factory.

Of course, my Grandad did not spring out of bed with gay abandon and did in fact shuffle off the mortal coil not long after.

 I had delicately mumbled my goodbyes and pondered out loud if I should wish him good luck to no answer. By this point he was so high on pain meds, I really don't think he gave a fuck who we were or what we were saying.

Watching a loved one have the light slowly snuffed out, in my opinion has got to be the most depressing death of them all. They want to go, you sort of want them to go, and then they finally do, and no one ever wants to talk about the *relief.*

Mum said that's because upon the news that Grandad had finally been put out of his misery I'd exclaimed loudly 'Well, thank fuck for that', but as I skulked off after a bollocking, I still thought I'd only said what everyone else was thinking.

Now, as an adult, I am not afraid of death, I'm also not afraid to speak about it, to be brutal and honest. I'm not afraid of doing that in life either. I just wish everyone else would get the memo.

If you are someone who would like to tiptoe around the subject, who believes that we should only speak about the dead with respect, in hushed tones and with a positive spin…

Then *this book is absolutely not for you.* Save me the shitty review and go speak to your pastor, or counsellor, or hippy life doula, or your own bloody diary.

This book is going to cover grief, the highs and lows, remembering that the people we lose are as multifaceted, difficult and irritating as they were when they were living. We can grieve all the aspects of the people will lose, and we should do so without shame or fear of judgement.

As such, when I looked at grief for the hundredth time, when my own Dad had suddenly dropped off the face of the Earth – I thought – *there's a book in that.*

Chapter 2 - The Phone Call

It is the most hateful thing, waiting for a phone call.

It is considerably more hateful waiting for a phone call to tell you that your Dad is dead. If that sounds depressing, it is because it is.

Every phone-call this week answered by me has received a blunt, short non-conversation. I am actively despising who-ever is daring to bother me, to wish me well, to 'just check in'.

Ryan has taken over; his responses are much more polite.

Bugger off, all of you.

They are all waiting, just like me. But they also want news, gossip, they want to know the gory details. I know, because I've done it too. We've all done it, haven't we? We hear whispers of some sudden accident, or rumour or salacious gossip and immediately hop in line to hear the latest juicy instalment of Someone Else's Life.

'You're not yourself,' I hear them say, before I curtly cut them off and return to my comfortable silence. No, it's not quite silence. The television plays in the background quietly, the hum of the fridge is still there. The pad of pawprints across the kitchen floor as one of the cats does the rounds to see if their bowls have been filled yet. My daughter, Lily, plays with her toys. Rain thrums against the windows gently, so no – silence doesn't return as such. It's comfort though, the comforting sounds of home. My home. Everyone doing what they should be. The heartbeat of this home is still intact. It brings me great comfort indeed.

But each time I hear that insipid ringtone, tearing through my comfortable home noise - my heart falls through my body. Waiting, waiting, waiting for the news. The news that will change everything.

I'm certain I'll know. I'll know when the change has happened.

I thought I'd feel an integral part of me float away. A chink in my soul. A missing piece, suddenly noticeable. A tangible hole somewhere about my person. A weight lifted. An intuitive knowing.

But I didn't.

The phone rings again, and I glare out the window.

Another time waster I presume, watching the pigeons' flap about on the cedar tree outside. I pick at some chipped paint on the windowsill, trying not to listen but wanting to hear at the same time. The paint flicks under my nail sharply and draws blood. I squeeze the end of my finger morbidly. A dome of blood swells to the tip, before the surface pressure breaks and it spills down my finger.

'OK' Ryan assures the stranger at the other end. 'I'll tell her.'

My ears prick up.

Ryan, my fiancé, the person whom I have chosen to do life with. The person who makes me laugh the most, and I claim every laughter line on his face as mine too. He is my rock, my soulmate and father to our beautiful daughter Lily. I didn't believe in love at first sight, but then I saw him. Cringe all you like, I don't care. When you know, you know – and I knew the instant I laid my eyes on him.

And now, this is it. His voice cuts through my thoughts. He begins to try to find the words, but he doesn't need to. The look on his face says it all.

Dad has gone.

'G, that was-'

'I know,' I say it bluntly. Jutting my chin out. I'd fold my arms, but my finger is throbbing painfully. As though I'm trying to convince everyone and myself that I'd known all along. He doesn't need to say it. His eyes work around my face, trying to see what I want, what I might need. I don't know myself.

Two arms wrap around me, enveloping me into his chest, squeezing the breath out of me. He rests his chin on my head and I, well, I sort of force it out. Proper ugly crying, the sort you can only do when something truly terrible has happened. And it has.

My Dad, my Daddy – is dead.

The life as I knew it has ended, it feels as though the world been whipped out from under me, and the only thing keeping me on it are the strong arms holding me here, trying their best to shelter me from the storm.

'When?' It's the only word I can get out, wet and muffled into Ryans jumper.

I probe the last half hour of non-events to see if I'd simply missed it. There must have been a hint, or maybe I was being too miserable to notice. I was so certain I would feel it, some all-knowing twang of a heartstring snapping. But I hadn't known. I hadn't felt a thing. It's been days since I saw Dad in hospital. Days since I knew this time he wouldn't come home. He wasn't going to make it. 'It's a waiting game.' the nurse had explained to me.

Just one with a really shitty prize at the end.

'About two hours ago.' Ryan interrupts my thoughts again. 'He had someone with him, your mum said. So, he wasn't alone.'

He's trying his best to be gentle, to offer me some support. My heart swells with love, but it feels like a hole has been punctured through, letting it all drain out again.

I can feel a lump in my throat, like someone has stuffed a dry sponge down there. I try to swallow it back, urge myself to form some words around it. A second word manages to squeeze past the choking feeling. 'Who?' *Who?* I didn't know. Ryan doesn't know either, he didn't think to ask. All I know is*, it wasn't one of us.* None of his close family holding his hand as he went. Too busy. All of us with life going on, and none of us sure we wanted to wait for it. *Or wait with him.* I'm bereft with the thought. I hate us all for that.

But - I think to myself miserably - I hate me the most.

There was no relief with this one. There'd been too much hope, that it was another of Dad's *incidents*. Another chance. Not this time. He'd had his run. The lives had run out. I can't bear to think about it.

I feel Ryan's concerned gaze on the side of my face and realise I'm frowning deeply at the fireplace. He's released me from his grip, not before I managed to empty the contents of my nose onto his jumper. 'It's fine,' He whispers to me, whilst I'm trying to apologise for the snail trails of tears and snot, he's now covered in. 'I don't care.'

I busy myself immediately, my method of self-soothing. Cleaning, tidying, wiping things down. Obsessive Compulsive Disorder, which always rears its head when I'm stressed. Out of control. Feeling vulnerable. It blurs my reality, almost a form of disassociation. My brain telling me to compete a ritual to regain control when I don't know what else to do.

It doesn't feel like that though. My brain doesn't say. 'Ritual, now!' It's more of a creeping urge to do something, that releases whatever hormone that makes me feel at ease again.

I don't realise I'm doing it most of the time, it's like my brain flicks to autopilot, and I've no control over what happens next. It feels just the same as when you notice a coating of dust on a cabinet, and absentmindedly wipe it away – only for me, I look up and I've got a toothbrush in my hand, and I've just been scrubbing some floor tiles for three hours.

Ryan catches me mid-swipe of dust from the top of the television, usually he would tell me to stop, to rest, to chat. But he knows I need to fill the void by staying busy. He knows me so well. We can have a full conversation without uttering a word to each other if we need to. His stormy eyes are talking to me now, and I hope mine find the words that my mouth can't.

I scoop Lily up and carry her to her bedroom. The centre of my world is wrapped up in this tiny being. My perfect daughter. My Raison D'Etre.

She's heavy in my arms and I kiss her head as I lay her gently into her bed. She smiles at me, her eyes twinkling. I can see myself in her eyes, despite them being *her* dads shape and colour. So full of love.

I have my dad's eyes. Or, I suppose it is now 'had'. Oh, it's happening already. Dad has gone from *is* and *does*, to *was* and *did*.

Another round of tears gathers on my eyelashes as I wonder what she understands of this whole situation. She is blissfully unaware that her Grandad is dead. Death, I suppose – for a three-year-old, is just too heavy to understand. I know 40-year-olds who have the same trouble.

I wonder if I should tell her or not.

I look at her beautiful innocent face gazing up at me and decide against it.

She didn't know her Grandad. He didn't-

Nope. I can't do it; I can't pick at that particular scab. It's too sore tonight.

The lump instantly returns, choking me as I kiss Lilys head again and turn her night light on. She can be swaddled in ignorance for now, this is something for me to deal with privately. When it's time, then she'll know.

Dad's gone, and now he'll miss out on all of this. Fresh tears drive down my cheeks again. I feel as though there's a tsunami of grief about to hit our household, about to wash me out the front door. We are only at the warning signs now – the water is retreating. How on Earth am I going to protect us all from the storm about to hit?

I have no idea. The thought is so overwhelming, I sit down behind Lilys bed and close my eyes tight. *What now, what now, what now?* I feel like I can hear the blood in my ears, my throat feels so tight I almost can't breathe.

'Do you want a cup of tea?' Ryan asks, poking his head around the door.

The vice loosens in my neck, and my head snaps up. Ryan wiggles his non-existent eyebrows at me.

'God, I thought you'd never ask.'

Chapter 3 – Death Admin

Death Admin.

What a delightful chore.

I offered to help with the organising of everything, mainly because I'd read it helps with the grieving process, a term which I am beginning to think ought to be written in inverted commas.

The 'Grieving Process'.

I am an organiser. I like things to have their place and make sense. It gives me comfort and feels safe. The 'Grieving Process' is something to be learned about, implemented and dealt with, so Life Can Go On.

Only, I don't want Life to Go On, because we are one incredibly important person down, and life simply Cannot Go On, without him. Yes, everything is in capitals now too.

Life Before this, and Life After.

Life-After, feels like a Life-Sentence. A ball and chain I've been lumbered with, expected to continue my day-to-day activities whilst I slug it about.

I feel petty and childlike, and wonder if this is also part of the 'Grieving Process'.

Naturally I have been awake at all hours researching, organising and finding data on how to grieve so it can be done efficiently, properly and without mess.

I felt similar when Lily was born. Life simply halted. It was a strange in-between time then. A limbo-land as life transitioned from one chapter to the next. No life before or after, instead life had just stopped, for a moment. I closed the curtains on the outside world and my tiny cherub became my whole world. I forgot that life existed outside our tiny nest, nothing happened beyond the sofa with the babe and Ryan curled up with me. Nothing important anyway. Everything I needed lived on our sofa-nest, with occasional refreshing of supplies. Nothing else mattered. Life simply did not happen. It had paused, and blissfully so.

Now, I demand it to halt. No one is to carry on past this point. No one can experience anything. Life must grind to a halt for everyone. Life would never be able to return to how it was, just as it hadn't when Lily had been born. There was 'Before Lily' life - but it felt out of focus and unreachable again now. We could never go back to what life had been before she was here. Neither did we want to. I could remember it, but it was hazy. I knew now, I was at another transition point, but this time I didn't want to move into the next stage.

I didn't want to leave Dad in the hazy, unreachable memories. I wanted him here, in the bright future side of life.

Oh bugger, I can feel tears rising again. They stream down my cheeks for the fifth time today. I've stopped wiping my face, as it's getting sore. I just let the tears fall now. I feel just as tragic and dramatic as that sentence looks.

I have googled how much you can cry in a day, then ended up in a 4am scroll hole before ending on a HuffPost Article cheerfully named *'13 Things You Probably Didn't Know About Tears.'*

I have strong suspicions that my tears were of sheer exasperation at this point.

However, my research was not all in vain, as I have learned that there are five stages of grief.

Denial, Anger, Bargaining, Depression and Acceptance.

I have achieved them all before 11am today.

Well, not the last one.

Acceptance.

I've read up on it, how you will eventually feel as though life is returning to normal. 'A new normal' it says. I scrunch my nose at the thought. *Nothing will ever feel normal again.*

Acceptance, I read on, is 'a newfound ability to acknowledge the reality of your loss and to allow sorrow and joy to live alongside one another. In this stage of grief, you're no longer immobilized by your sadness.'

How could I ever?

How does anyone ever?

The task seems impossible, an Everest. A never-ending hole that simply can't be filled and will therefore suck in all my happiness in from now, until forever.

I curse my stupid father for taking my happiness away from me, from Ryan, from Lily. From everyone that loves me. My core personality trait is my joy of life, no matter what. My everlasting optimism. And my sardonic comments, but mainly the bright shine of hope that has never ever been extinguished.

That was my first tattoo – '*There is always hope.*' It's one of the only ones that actually has any meaning. I felt it so strongly I wanted it etched in view, forever. There *was* always hope. I'd believed it so resolutely. There hadn't been a single situation I'd been in that felt so hopeless that I'd given up. Not yet. That little flame in me that keeps me pushing on, keeps me optimistic. Something will happen, something will help.

Now Dad has ripped it away by going and bloody dying before his time. By not reaching out, by taking himself off to- I kick one of Lilys toys in frustration. I would never leave her like this, *I would never do this to my child.* A rage burns inside me, this emotion that I am so not used to feeling. I'm seething, irritable and hateful. He did this to me, he chose this.

Selfish. Selfish. Selfish.

The word burns on my tongue, but I can't bring myself to say it. I don't feel like I can talk to anyone about this, even Ryan feels out of reach. I feel so unlike me, I'm not sure how to get me back. I want to tear the room apart. To rip up his photographs and smash anything that reminds me of him. I want to reach into my mind; to grab all the questions I so desperately want to ask him and squeeze them into oblivion. That's all they are good for now; I'll never ever know the answers. He took those too.

I throw myself down onto the sofa and the penny drops.

That's Anger, done for another hour.

Back to the admin chores. Back to organising and sorting, to feel pragmatic feels like a plaster over this gaping wound. It's not a permanent one, but it'll stem the flow for a moment.

When Dad left this earthly realm, he had £33.10 in one account, and a single £1 in the other. I know, because I closed the accounts and sent the money on to cover the funeral costs.

A drop in the ocean.

It hurt, to see all that he owned in the world. But it was also a bit pathetic. All that life, and all he had left was £34.10. Not even enough for a good takeaway.

It hurt more when I contacted the bank to tell them Dad had snuffed it, to receive half hearted 'sorry for your loss' and then receive a letter addressed to 'Park', instead of Mark. I crumpled the letter up; despite being told I'd have to keep it all, in my Death Admin folder. It went in the log burner not long after.

Ryan and I had gone to see Dad's earthly belongings on the day of the funeral. We'd been instructed to take whatever we wanted that day, anything left would be disposed of. The moment the garage door rattled open; the smell of Dad hit me in the face. His familiar earthy, gardener smell.

It's always surprised me how the smell of something can transport you back to a time, place or person.

Nina Ricci perfume reminds me of my friend Laura, of scary London visits, whilst I tried to be cooler than I was, as we travelled to Soho, me for the first time. I can feel the bittersweet taste of chocolate vodka we'd drank on the train; I was taking half-sips because I was too nervous to want to actually be drunk, but still wanted to have a cool and unbothered air about such things.

The smell of Dettol and green soap makes me shiver with cold, as I'm tattooed for hours, the collection of them now extensive, sweat prickling my armpits as I pretend this *sooooo* doesn't hurt, even though I want to kick my dear friend Cat in the face after about five minutes as she drags a harsh dry wipe over my injured skin.

The sweet smell of childhood summer – hot tarmac, cut grass, lavender fields and sickly-sweet honeysuckle drifting through the window at bedtime, even though it's still light outside.

And now, this garage, so full of Dad but with him nowhere to be found.

I'd looked around, but it was so painful. Each item brought a fresh stab to my chest. His prized records on the damp floor, boxes of books and crockery, his gardening tools scattered around. His woollen gardening jacket, the bright autumnal oranges and reds woven through it now seemed dull. The sleeves empty. It looked so sad without him filling it. I could smell the woodsmoke on it as I brushed past. I could feel the softness as I leant my head against his arm, stopping to look at the view somewhere during a late September walk. Feel his hand slip into mine, or that familiar 'pat' of affection as we watched deer drink from a river and chimney smoke spiral over the trees. I wanted to hold the jacket now, and for him to be here telling me, 'It's alright, Jelly.'

The pang of my nickname and following thought that I'd never hear it again was too much too soon, especially to be faced with a garage of Dad just after leaving him in a box to be burnt away.

And now we were here, picking over his things that weren't worth anything, but had also just become priceless artefacts.

They were removed a few days later. I took nothing. It was too much, to find The Item to remember him, and forgo all the rest. They were all his things, but nothing really *spoke* of him. I'd wanted a true Dad item but had felt so overwhelmed I'd been unable to choose.

So, I had nothing.

I regretted it now, not taking a book or something poignant. I'd been handed some photographs from Dad's friends at the wake. And given a letter he'd written to his friend Simon back in 2000.

But I hadn't been brave enough to read it, not even during Grief Hour. I felt it wouldn't be conducive to my strict time keeping, a threat to blow Grief Hour over to Grief Day – then what? It would be too much to keep a lid on, to fool everyone that I was doing fine! My Dad's dead! But Life Goes On!

I didn't have any belongings from childhood either, when Ryan and I had arrived in Cornwall with our clothes, a car and a duvet - we always thought we'd go back for the rest, but it always felt like we had the rest of our lives to worry about that.

Then, not long before Dad died, he'd been evicted from our family home, but he hadn't told anyone until D-Day, so no one had any time to rescue anything. Mum had attempted to get some things, but they'd been Toms photos, and an art folder full of scraps. She'd wanted to be a support for Dad more than anything, not able to pick over things before he was chucked out. Anything left had landed in the tip.

I'd not been able to save anything for Lily to inherit.

The lump threatens to rise again. Getting rid of his worldly possessions was such a clear forewarning of what was to come, what he was -

I can't think it, the lump pushes up my throat like a dry golf ball, sitting painfully behind my tonsils. Not ready.

It makes me want to gag, retch, or cough it out. But I can't.

I'm not ready to talk about it, I'm not ready to think about it.

It was an accident, I tell myself. The denial releases the lump of grief, and it sinks lower until I can swallow again.

An accident. Mismanagement. Misadventure.

That's what the coroner said.

Chapter 4 - The Funeral

The funeral was on a Friday.

I had the bright idea to wear lots of make-up, so I wouldn't allow myself to cry it all off and so everyone would think I was doing great. What a bizarre notion. But I was already feeling invisible pressure to clear the decks after the funeral and continue with life as normal.

Grief was too uncomfortable for everyone else to keep dragging it out beyond that. No one had said that to me, not a single person, but I felt they didn't need to. *It was implied.* 'Just get through the funeral, and you'll be okay.' 'You've got Lily to focus on, that's what is important.' 'You need to think about how Grandma must feel, it's a completely different thing to lose a child.' Each comment had felt double edged, some obvious, others I searched for hidden meaning. Confirmation that grief was to be expected, dumped out at the funeral and then burnt with the coffin.

Then life must continue.

It was quite the turn-out, that's what you are supposed to say isn't it? 'Quite the turn-out'. Lots of on-lookers, some to say goodbye to a childhood friend, a brother, an acquaintance. Some perhaps to make sure the fucker was dead.

As we drove into the crematorium, Ryan said that we seemed to visit here too often. I was halfway through saying 'Perhaps we should ask for our own parking space-' when Grandma walked out of the crowd and nearly kissed the car bonnet.

My aunt came shooting out moments later to shepherd her back to safety. 'She's got dementia!' I could hear her trilling over the heads of people who'd looked over to witness the imminent tragedy. 'Dementia!' I waved at Grandma who looked meekly back, and I thought I saw a glimmer of embarrassment.

Yes, she did have the early stages of dementia, I knew, already - Grandma and I kept in contact via regular letters.

Post-Grandad I'd decided to send her post that didn't include a deepest sympathies, bills or reminders that *pensions don't last forever when you insist on shopping at Waitrose'*. I thought she might enjoy some old-fashioned letter writing, and so we had begun writing to each other. It had become a thrice-a-year habit.

I'd noticed as her letters had become shorter, more sporadic, and often filled of nothing more than weather updates. Which meant mine had to answer questions that hadn't been asked, and sounded more and more like a reading from an Enid Blyton extract as I tried to glaze over her obvious bewilderment at why the world didn't work how she was used to. *'Oh yes, Grandma – we had a frightfully jolly time at the beach last week, Lily built a sandcastle, and we foraged for shells to decorate it.'*

Yes, she had dementia, I thought glumly as my aunt was using the 'She's got dementia!' trill as a tool to get to the front of the crowd, pushing a more and more downtrodden Grandma through the fold first. *She's not deaf yet though.*

As we pulled up, one of Dad's friends, Sarah, came out of the suddenly overwhelming crowd of people waving and beckoning to us. They were a sea of faces, and frankly, I wanted nothing more than to get straight back in the car. I was still holding the car handle and debating getting back in when she swept me up into a hug, words of support whispered kindly into my ear.

'I know it's overwhelming, but you've got this. Your Dad would be proud that you are here.'

Sarah had joined the Dead Dad Club years previous, at 21. Even younger than me. She must be in her fifties now, although I didn't want to ask and didn't like to guess. She'd gone to school with Dad, and they'd reconnected a few years ago. She was a powerhouse, blonde and beautiful, cool and interesting. If Sarah said I could do this, then she was right. I was grateful for her all-consuming hug, her sweet words of belief. It was exactly what I needed. I straightened my dress, gave Ryan the nod, and we walked into the crowd hand in hand.

It was like a film premiere, I thought darkly to myself, a small smile growing. This was the part of Death that thrilled me. *The attention seeking, vain me.* Dad's funeral had - for a brief moment - become all about me. People clamouring over themselves to shake our hands, to say hello, to ask how we were, apart from the obvious. People from each stage of my life, from tiny infant to the grown woman I was now.

They wanted to know where Lily was, how was she doing? *It's so great to see how happy you all are.* Your Dad would be so proud. The old man this, the old man that. I shook hands, made jokes and compared heights with the 'kids', only now we have all grown up and the boys I used to tower over are now towering over me. I feel sick with myself for enjoying it.

Everything seemed to be happening in a blur, before I realise - *they are all waiting for me* – succession, I guess. Was I the matriarch replacing Dad in his role?

The dry sponge appears back in my throat, and I try to swallow it down. Ryan finds my hand through the crowd and gives it a reassuring squeeze.

'Right then...' I say loudly, and everyone goes quiet. They all look to me expectantly. My mind goes blank as the silence cloaks the crowd, and I realise I have no idea what to say or which direction to point them all in. I see movement behind me and see it is the hearse pulling up, with a white coffin in the back.

'Here he is.' One of Dads friends says quietly.

Everyone seems to have the same thought, and the loud crowd of laughing, joking, exclamations of this or that has died down to a sombre silence. I feel those tears I'd been so desperate to fight back begin to pinch the corner of my eyes. Soberly, the celebrant opens the back door and asks me who is carrying the coffin.

God, I have no idea. I'd been completely pushed out of organising the funeral by my aunt and sister. I'd just rolled over and let them, not ready to take the lead, or more importantly – argue with each other them – both were powerhouses in different ways. It would be like trying to take on Ann Robinson and Vicky Pollard at the same time.

Speaking of the devil, my sister pushes through the crowd, a face like thunder. That's not that unusual if you know my sister, but empathy rises for her. Anger is the first emotion for her when things are stressful. And, well – I've never attended a funeral that didn't have emotions running high.

She takes over the coffin organising, literally standing on my toes to do so and my brother is shunted forward as a carrier of the coffin.

The trouble is, he's a short-arse, so whilst there is reassembling and organising of height differences amongst Dad's friends to ensure that his son can carry him in, I can feel the lump in my throat, which hasn't really disappeared since it found its initial spot a few weeks ago, but now it feels like a tumour – growing larger by the moment, a horrible cancer that is threatening to choke me. I battle it back, clearing my throat as Ryan uses my arse to push me forward into the chapel.

Clair pushes through again, sitting firmly at the front – my Mum, Aunt and Grandma sitting beside them. It feels pointed, but I just don't care. If that's what they need for today, then let them have it.

Ryan takes my other side; he's holding some napkins stolen earlier from a café. 'Just in case' he winks to me, casting doubt on my heavily made-up plan to not cry at my own Dad's funeral.

My brother is last, throwing himself down so violently in the pew that even Uncle Jay can't hold in a 'Fucking hell Tom! Just making sure ey?'

A waft of alcohol follows him, and I realise he is absolutely twatted. It seems that Tom has his own plan to get through today. My heart breaks a little for him, as I want to reach over Ryan and hold his hand, but a shyness stops me. He and Ryan begin chattering as everyone else does, the room filling with the buzz of old friends catching up, comments on the architecture, I catch a glimpse of my Aunt leaning over Grandmas lap to tell Mum, again, that Grandma 'has got dementia.' Everyone is doing something to steer off the melancholy of the days subject.

Me though, I can't take my eyes off the box.

The coffin, I correct myself.

Morbid curiosity rises to reach the lump, that has now – thankfully - subsided enough I can swallow again, but not quite disappeared completely and I'm reminded of a friend years ago telling me that people can go so mad with grief they try to get in the coffin with their dearly departed.

He's in there. I tell myself.

I picture myself walking over, and lifting the lid to peer in.

I'd missed the chance yesterday – due to travelling – to put something in with him. My Aunt had taken over that bit, kindly offering to 'put in a packet of biscuits? As he always had them on him.'

Ryan had scoffed when I read that email out, pointing out that the reason Dad always had biscuits with him was because he was diabetic.

Dad had hated his diabetes so much, always feeling tied down. It had been his own heavy cross to bear. Never able to be spontaneous in the way the rest of us could. Always monitored by blood sugar or food types. He'd shown me a diary of his, from when he was about 7 years old. First diagnosed, feeling like nothing would ever be the same again. And he'd told me, privately – it wasn't.

It had been a quiet moment, between the two of us, and I'd felt honoured that he'd chosen to share that with me, letting me pore over the pages in this beaten-up old diary he'd written as a young, frightened kid.

My Dad, the free-spirited, organic-loving, permanently-outside, weather-beaten old hippy-punk. It was hard to ever imagine him being tied down by anything, but he'd made the admission to me nearly a decade ago. I hadn't forgotten. It changed my view of his regimented ways, his need for control over the household. That was something he was in control of, whereas his illness made him feel like he wasn't in control of anything. I wondered now, if he had been trying to reveal something to me, that he hadn't been able to just say.

Mum had slipped a bit of our cat Parsley's fur in with him. Clair had put in some letters from her kids, and a photo or two. My Aunt had put in a shirt of his, and the bloody biscuits.

Tom had slipped in a spliff, sniggering as he told Ryan.

Dad was about to be cremated, so it would be one last high as he went out.

He's in there.

I was finding it incredibly distracting, as people began to speak about him. Everyone was being very formal, and I couldn't help a smirk finding its way onto my face. Dad would have hated it– I could just picture him flicking the V's at the whole scenario in his box.

His coffin.

He's in there.

Mum got up to speak, talking about how he was the father of her kids, and something about forgiveness and memories and peace at last. I just couldn't pick up anything else, it just felt like white noise all around me.

He's in there.

Clair trailed after Mum, went to speak but couldn't. Mum read out the poem for her. I took my eyes off them and back to Dad.

What does he 'look' like in there?

I look around to see if anyone has noticed, I feel like my thoughts are so loud someone must be able to hear them.

Grandma gets up to read another poem, which is then yanked out of her hands and read out for her. She stumbles on the last step down, and a trill of 'Oh, Mum! Careful now!' follows her.

Ryan started sniggering. I squeeze his leg before I started going too. I wasn't unconvinced that the sniggers may turn into tears, and I didn't fancy leaving the chapel looking like Alice Cooper. Dad's band had been named just that – *'Careful, now!'* It was poetic in a way I couldn't quite describe.

Then Tom got up. My twin brother. Twin bother, sometimes.

My Aunt and Grandma didn't hide how appalled they were at what he was wearing, which whilst scruffy, also looked like it hadn't been taken off for around two years. Which, knowing my brother, may have been true.

He cleared his throat and began.

'Everyone here knew my Dad, in one way or another.' He paused and looked around, some fidgeting and sniffs filling the pregnant pause.

'Some of you knew him as Mark,' he clears his throat, trying to talk a bit louder. My brother, the mumbler. He fiddles with the light at the podium. Fiddly Tom. All of the idiosyncrasies coming out to play, making my grown-up brother look like the little boy I grew up with. It makes my heart ache, and I try not to dwell there. 'Mark Potten... Some of you knew him as Dirty, some as Stevie-P, some as D-'

As my brother was delivering his speech, and the endless nicknames that Dad had had, someone leant forward and whispered in my ear *'I go by many names'* in his sagest of voices. I couldn't hold the giggle in, and spun round to see Callum, his brother Harry, and Dad's best friends - Smurf and Max, all beaming at me. It was a Mighty Boosh joke, something we had all shared back in 2008, and now 10 years later, we were all giggling about it at Dads funeral.

Tom continued, telling all of us in his bouncing tone – no matter in which capacity we knew him, no matter what the status our relationships were with him when he left us. We had all known and loved him in our own way. And all that mattered now was that we were all here, together – to say goodbye. That was the final honour.

It struck me then, that this boy – my brother – perhaps knew Dad the best. Perhaps had the closest final relationship with him. Didn't care for family spats, or pecking order, or anything else. He had no need for getting that in there, for establishing his role as Head of the Mourners. He didn't feel the noise, or anger or anything else that the rest of us were prickling with today.

He saw it as simply as it was, that we had all lost the same man. And that was enough of a tragedy, without a family arguing too.

He always had a knack for that, did my brother.

I mean, we used to argue – all of us, I mean, not just Tom and me.

Our family was as dysfunctional as they come. We'd had fights that meant belongings being thrown up and down the stairs, spitting on each other, hitting each other. Finding words that would hurt the most – and to be honest, often it was Dad found at the eye of the storm. But my brother, Mister Switzerland. Jimmy Neutral. *Mr Not-Getting-Involved.*

I'd admired him for that, although I was often jealous and spiteful over it too. Being unable to switch off my need for having my voice heard loudest over the shouting, for the last thing that smashed on the wall to have left my hands. Whilst Dad may have loved to start it, I always wanted to be the one to 'finish it'.

And Mr Swiss and Swede would glide through the chaos, find solace in his bedroom and make us all feel a bit foolish for getting swept up in the drama.

So really, he ended it.

Tom finishes his beautiful speech and introduces a song he has chosen for this moment. As the music filters through the speakers dotted around the room, a tendril of ice pierces through me. 'Anthony and the Johnsons - Hope There's Someone', begins to fill up the empty space and I think to myself, *Tom you bastard. I'll never be able to listen to this song again.*

I look at my brother, who shuffles back to his seat, to pats on the back from those nearest to him, before returning my eyes back to the coffin.

He's in there.

Despite all our dysfunction, our fighting and cruel words. Dad had been our glue. He'd forced us together, to 'suck it up' and be pleasant to one another. He'd berate all of us and tried to guide us to being 'the decent human beings I know you can be'.

And now he had gone.

And my brother and sister and I – despite having the same upbringing, by the same two people – couldn't be more different. Now we were three lost adults with nothing in common.

Was this it? I thought about it. All these people who had played such a huge part of my life – was this goodbye to all of them too? The lump rises up and I feel like I'm chewing on it.

The endless expanse of loss was more than I'd ever felt before. I close my eyes. Don't cry. Don't cry. *Don't fucking cry.*

Ryans hand brushed mine, and I felt him pressing a stolen napkin into it. The wordless kindness was too much, and tears began to gather in the corners of my eyes. I dabbed at them in a way I hoped was rather nonchalantly. To my surprise, a smile took shape on my lips…

What sort of mental health issue do I have that I am so desperately concerned with not crying at my own father's funeral? If I can't cry now, then really – when could I?

I couldn't explain it, but the thought was so amusing that I had to bite my lip to stop another giggle filtering out.

My Aunt then invited us up to write on the coffin. I realised it was white, because it was fresh cardboard – and she offered out a pen pot, not unlike one you'd find at a nursery, for us all to write our condolences on.

Everyone began to filter around the coffin like a buffet table, no one wanting to be the first to write anything, perhaps not sure what to say. Beanie, one of Dads closest friends thrust a pen into my hand. 'Go on…' he offered, gently.

I looked to Ryan, who nodded me on too. I could hear my heartbeat in my ears. It's like the room is spinning and everyone has blurred together. I grip the pen tighter. Forcing down the last memory of being unable to say how I really felt before he-

I can't go there, not now. There are too many eyes on me. Pressure to write the first word, to set the stage for everyone else to pour out their grief. To say something apt, heartfelt, true, loving.

I see the gold plaque on top.

Mark Johnathon Potten.

1966-2018.

Age 52 years.

Is that it? I think, lip curling at the thought.

A lifetime, a boy, a man. Brother. Cousin. Father. Grandad. Friend. Lover.

All summed up and written off in those short words. Name, Age. Date. For God's sake.

I struggle to click the lid off the pen, my hands are betraying me. I've got no grip. I think, I'll never be able to demonstrate my fabulous handwriting now. Another thought immediately crashes into that one and hisses at me, *no one cares about your fucking handwriting now.* I swallow the lump down again, but it rests dangerously on the precipice of my throat. My thoughts are all over the place. I lean forward to write something, anything – but I can't think straight.

My hand comes into view, as I reach a shaky hand towards my dad's coffin-

He's in there.

He's in there.

He's in there.

My heart thumps loudly, white noise fills my ears. I feel as though all my thoughts have been replaced my angry question marks. Say something. Write something. Do something. I urge myself to do it.

The sound of a felt-tip being pressed too hard screeches near my ear. I look down first, to see if it's my body on autopilot, slightly curious to see what my hands will scribe without the engagement of my brain – then to my left, following the movement of hands - and see my sister and niece scrawling something on the top of the coffin. A glance at Ryan and I can see he feels it too.

Not allowed to help with the funeral. *Let the adults do it.*

Not allowed to say anything. *There won't be enough time after everyone else.*

Not able to put anything in the coffin. *I'll do it for you, but you'll have to tell me what.*

Not allowed to choose the music. *That's really for Tom to do.*

Not allowed to help carry the coffin. *That's for the men to do.*

Not allowed to plan the wake. *We'll ask you for ideas but choose none of them.*

I pass my pen to someone behind me and stand on the steps to take a breather.

My Aunt sidles up to us. 'Oh, I love doing this, it's great isn't it?'

Ryan can't help himself this time, leaning around me, he asks incredulously, 'Being at a funeral?'

'Well, you know, the organising, the speaking, the ideas – do you like the drawing idea? Your Dad was so creative, I think he'd have quite liked it.'

During her speech she'd told a story she'd regaled once before at Christmas. The story is about some bottles of cola, or milk or something. The punchline is, she tricked Dad into believing that when the bottles were empty, the colour on the bottom changed. She found it hilarious to tell everyone that when Dad thought she wasn't looking – she saw him check the bottoms of the bottles. Gullible, bumbling idiot that he is!

When Dad was here, he had been staunch that the story hadn't happened like this at all. He'd looked at the bottom of one as the glass bottom was reflective. It all sounds petty now, but Dad hated that story, hated the way his sister had gleefully made the whole room take him for an idiot, and now she was telling it again – at his funeral – he couldn't argue against it. The final speech, the final moment for everyone to take with them. He was a fool, and now he's a dead fool.

I could feel the lump rising again, but this time it was met with something else. Anger. This wasn't grief anger; this wasn't going to subside and be replaced with another emotion. This was the sort of anger that follows something unfair.

The feeling when you are punished for something you haven't done.

Wanting to stand up for someone, who can't do it for themselves.

Blamed for something you can't prove wasn't you.

Written off for being something less when you are more than.

Truth twisting, finger-pointing, pointless power trip – unfairness.

I'd felt it so many times before, and now – embarrassingly, all I could do in response was to cry. Words would fail me, actions felt fruitless. I just wanted to howl until everyone went away.

Ryan bundled me out the back door, first guiding me back to scrawl something quickly on the coffin.

'Love, light and peace, Goodbye Dad'. How Dad ended his letters, his emails and anything else handwritten. It wasn't enough, but it was everything as well.

Uncle Jay was outside smoking. Tom was with him, gesticulating wildly. Deep in the middle of some story.

Grateful for the faces of the sane, ironically considered the two nutters of the family, two black sheep of two very different and yet so similar family units.

More people began to join, and we found ourselves swept in the tide of people walking back to their cars ready to join the wake. Mum and Clair in front, Grandma floating around. Ryan and my brother. Me and Uncle Jay, the sway of familiarity like so many other walks before, it could have been a Christmas a few decades ago. Gentle conversation flowed and I stopped Jay. 'Oh wait, Where's Dad? I want to speak to-'

Oh.

Of course.

He's in that box.

Jay looks at me kindly, patting my shoulder as we walk. Grief rises, sits in my throat, and fills my stomach with an encompassing heaviness that threatens to never leave me.

It won't, I think bitterly. I know this time, it won't go.

Chapter 5– Grief Hour

Sleep has been escaping me lately.

This time I'm woken by a dull ache in my jaw.

Between the cats padding through, the house settling for the night and Lily stirring – the 'Mum Ear' never turns off. I can sleep through a storm, probably a hurricane. I can ignore Ryans snores, tossing and turning. The cats can walk across my head and lick my eyelids and breathe their catty breath into my nostrils, but I can sleep for England. I love sleep, and sleep loves me. I could sleep standing up if I was tired enough. But if Lilys breath catches – I'm awake.

I think of the first night we brought her home, heeding everyone's warnings that 'you'll never sleep again', it had been cruelly drummed into us, over and over, (as though I was sleeping like the dead with a watermelon stuck to my front for several months) so, the two of us – exhausted by the day's events, stayed up – waiting for her to begin the campaign of 'No Sleep Again.'

But she slept soundly, unaware yet that she'd actually been born yet. The tenth month of pregnancy takes place outside of your body, I'd later learnt - swaddled and held by either me or her Daddy.

If we did put her down, we would lean over her bassinet, just staring until our eyes blurred. Trying to take every ounce of her in. Waiting for her to stir, to wail or cry.

But sleep, she did.

The night wakings began not long after that, of course, but honestly – we just took it in our stride. Ryan was on nappy duty, and I would feed her back to sleep. We had a system that worked as neatly as a Formula One Pit Stop, returning to sleep as quickly as possible was the Holy Grail. Childcare, I decided arrogantly - just needed an efficient system.

Eventually, she began to sleep for longer intervals – the first four-hour stretch made me feel like I had been reborn. I felt rejuvenated. It was as though I'd had a magic spell put on me, that had replenished my dull, pale skin. Removed the bags from my eyes, let my hair bounce and sway. Realising that I'd finally woken up of my own accord, I yawned, stretched and then immediately panicked that she was dead.

Ryan did the exact same, leaping over the bed to check the bassinet, but she was peacefully snoozing, her tiny chest rising and falling as it should.

That panic never leaves you. Even now, at three years old – if she sleeps in, we still shit ourselves.

Toothache interrupts my nostalgia, and I use my tongue to investigate. I probe each tooth, gently pushing against them to see if any have finally started to wobble.

I haven't been looking after myself, a guilty little voice tells me, and now it's finally happening.

My tongue discovers a tangy little divot, at the back of my mouth – a sharp edge fights back and my tongue retreats, and the finger goes in. In my own self-destructive way, I'd been hoping that not looking after my teeth would mean the little horrors fell out, so I could just get dentures instead.

It seems a strange request, but Dad had terrible teeth, replaced with dentures eventually. He'd come back from the dentist one day with these bright white Hollywood pearlers, standing out bone-white against his weather-beaten face. We'd joked at the time, that he ought to take them in to get 'browned up' a bit, so they'd suit him more. But secretly I'd been seething with jealousy and plotting how to rip my own horrible teeth out to get a fresh set of *those*.

I'd had lovely teeth as a kid, then they were replaced with my adult teeth that just seemed to grow in wrong. I was a dorky, lanky little thing. Pale skin set against deep brunette hair. Glasses always perched on my nose as I was always hunched over a book or drawing.

Nowadays it would probably be considered sweet, but no one ever used that word to describe me then.

Kids are bastards like that, and they picked on my glasses, my love of books and art, *and* my teeth until I left school.

I had a large gap in my front teeth, which, as a teenager, I would squirt water through to amuse my pals. Being funny was more important than being beautiful I'd decided, and as I couldn't change my appearance, I would settle for attention that way instead. Mum and Dad had always put great importance beauty being only skin deep, and to work on the inside, rather than the exterior. Neither of them understood not only my desire to look nice, but my persistent worry for what anyone else thought of me. 'Who cares what anyone else thinks?' Dad would say, genuinely surprised that anyone would consider this an issue. Mum didn't wear make-up either, so I couldn't pilfer anything from her to edit my looks, and other than his pearly whites (that didn't last long) Dad wouldn't have looked out of place with a coin-filled hat at his feet.

Of course, as an adult I understand they were trying to show me that what was on the outside is just the shell, and our inner selves will shine out regardless.

I'd asked them if I was pretty and Mum had helpfully supposed, after examining my face for a few minutes. 'You have... an interesting face.'

When I'd complained at this non-compliment, she'd explained - 'Well, there's a lot going on!'

Dad had later patted my knee reassuringly and told me – 'You have a beautiful smile'.

I'd peered in the mirror smiling like a crazed loon to confirm for myself, that in fact - my parents were Big Fat Liars.

As a result, I rarely looked after my teeth. I hated them, it didn't matter how clean they were – they looked like a broken fence, a Jaws tribute, and so on…. I'd heard them all. I liked to refer to them as 'freestyle' before someone else could.

I had finally gotten braces, at the unhappy age of eighteen. Unlike everyone else who can join the adult world with their smile worries long forgotten about… I had to find ways to sneak into pubs or clubs without ID, as the youngest of my friends – and 'train-track' braces were a dead cert to get carded. Try getting served in Wetherspoons with braces, it's a real hoot, I'm telling you.

I'd gotten through it, and less than a year later, they came off. My teeth were straight. I couldn't believe it. There had been talk of breaking jaws, and taking teeth out, but there was no need. The metal had worked. The gaps were closed. They all stood in line. Finally.

My NHS dentist polished them off and handed me a retainer. 'Wear this for six months' He'd said.

By month eight, my teeth had started to move back.

A year later, they were, as my dear friends put it. 'On the piss again.'

I gave up then, envious of anyone with straight white teeth, and settled into thinking – that was a blessing not destined for me. Other people were allowed to be pretty, I'd just have to make do.

Now, I was struggling through the days in a haze of grief, personal hygiene was even further down the list of priorities. I simply didn't care now. Dad had been right. The thought of vanity and appearance seemed like a pointless trait, and an unachievable goal. Trouble was, my award-winning personality had been snuffed out, which had left me an ugly, laugh-less miserable bint.

Now my jaw ached, which wasn't the desired outcome so I tried some home remedies until even paracetamol wouldn't touch it.

Fine. I'd have to go to the dentist. I shuddered at the thought.

*

The dentist peered in, and I braced myself for the lecture.

'Do you smoke?'

'No.'

'When did you last attend the dental surgery?'

Not since I was pregnant.'

'Which was?'

I point to Lily.

'Ahh.'

I shrug. Hoping my nonchalance about it all will act as a smokescreen for my embarrassment.

'Your wisdom teeth are impacted.' He explains, as though I know what that means. I nod along. 'I have referred you to the hospital to have them extracted under a general anaesthetic. They'll contact you.'

'Oh. Ok.'

'And, Miss Potten…' He looks over his ridiculously magnified glasses. 'I recommend an appointment with the hygienist; you have the beginnings of gum disease. If you act now, you can reverse it and save your teeth.'

I rolled my eyes, I bet they say that to everyone.

A few weeks later, my wisdom teeth have been whipped out.

I was knocked out with general anaesthetic, mid-conversation. The nurses had assured me they would count down and I'd know what to expect. That I would gently fall asleep as they reached '…One.' Instead, they'd been firing questions at me and as I searched my brain for an answer, I'd realised I was losing consciousness. My last shaky words as my body powered down had been an indignant 'You…tricked...me…'

When I woke up, with my face rearranged, I burst into tears.

A nurse looked over her magazine, tutted and threw a yoghurt down on my bedside table. 'Eat that.'

The yoghurt slopped onto the table; my mouth hurt too much to even open it. I wasn't hungry, despite being nil-by-mouth for over 24 hours now.

All I felt was pain, aching and tiredness. And the comforting pull of blackness on my back. I wondered briefly if that's what heroin feels like, and if it is – I'd be fucked, because I love that feeling. The way your bed pulls you back in on a cold morning. Maybe Death feels that way too. My eyes began to close again, and the nurse screeches at me across the room– 'No! You need to stay awake!'

Her voice was so curt and sharp, against my drowsy state, I burst into tears. Forcing myself awake, I text Ryan to come and save me. I hate hospitals. The last time I was in a hospital was when Dad-

No. Not now. I don't want to go there. I'm feeling too delicate. I close my eyes anyway, drowsiness taking over. Fuck that nurse. Shout at me, I don't care, I don't want to be here. Tears fall down my face and I disassociate completely from my surroundings. I tune out of the pain in my face, out of the pain of grief, and being frightened and fragile. The only thing that brings me back into the room is my phone buzzing against the table.

Ryan has replied. 'I'm on my way.'

A few days later, I trudge up to preschool to collect Lily. I still have pale heart monitor circles on my chest as I'd had the wise idea to fake tan myself before going under. I'd wanted to look nice, but had forgotten to pack slippers, so had to walk through the surgery wards in pop socks and my dirty trainers, feeling like my arse was on show in the little hospital nightie. I'd looked an orange fool.

My jaw is still swollen, my eyes have faint yellow bruises underneath and my nose is all puffy. I don't know who is looking back at me in the mirror, and I don't care to know her either.

Whilst Lily is at preschool, I write, I clean, I have Grief Hour.

After deciding to tackle grief like a project, I learned that crying all day was beginning to grate on everyone, myself included.

I'd burst into noisy tears at Lily's kids TV programmes. I'd see a robin and cry. I'd look on social media and cry at that. And if I wasn't crying, I was sleeping. Sometimes I'd wake up in the night for a little crying interlude then too. I felt pathetic.

I stopped blogging and sharing anything online. Writing just couldn't happen. I had been blocked, truly and finally. I didn't want to be perceived by anyone, including myself. It was all just too messy and raw and scary.

Instead, I had begun a self-imposed exile. Ryan would return home, and I'd cry again. I'd sit on the sofa, like a little grieving zombie, staring into space with no idea how I was ever going to be normal again.

So, I decided to be pragmatic and concentrate the grief into Grief Hour.

Grief Hour goes like this – I whizz around doing all the chores and life admin I need to, knowing that I can escape into Grief Hour as a morbid little treat.

Then I sit down, get out any photos I have, any letters and trawl Facebook for more. Now that's just picking at the Grief Scab. Then I get really into it and get my Grief Playlist going. The final song, Dad's funeral song, that is always the breaker.

I'd thought I'd never be able to listen to it again, how wrong I was! It has become my Grief Hour anthem.

Tears drip onto the photos, I repeat memories, ask questions I don't have answers to, and sob my pathetic little heart out.

Then my phone alarm signals that the hour is up, the book gets closed, the playlist is turned off, and it's time to get Lily.

And now, as I slope up to the preschool, one of the mums stops me.

'Are you OK? She asks me, her eyes are wide and searching my face. Her hand is clawing at my arm, attempting to pull me to the side. I want to yank it out of her grip, but it's been a second too long, so I look down at it and then back at her worried face.

'Yes, I'm fine?' I lie, confused at her bewilderment.

I catch a distorted version of my face in a car window, and realise – I have a bruised face, the same stained jumper I've thrown on for weeks, and tear streak marks down my swollen cheeks. I've been avoiding the school mum chit-chat since well, you know.

Oh.

'… I had my wisdom teeth out.' I sound muffled and cottony. Even my voice isn't mine anymore.

I attempt a smile, to reassure her, I can feel my lips tight against my face. Then I catch a glimpse of *that* face in the car window and stop immediately.

She lets go of my arm, and nods with a false smile – she must think I am having some sort of mental breakdown and has decided to save herself, in case it's catching.

I do like the School Mums, having known them for a couple of years. I can make idle chat, we've had picnics, and walks and other such mumsy things. But my self-imposed exile meant they were the first to go. I've waited out school drop-offs and pick-ups until the very last moment, so I can run in, grab my kid and run off again before someone can even finish the word 'Hello'.

I feel guilty now, wondering if they know I'm 'going through it' but not sure how to approach me. Or worse, they have no idea why I've decided to avoid them all like the plague.

I considered holding a plaque or making a sign to go around my neck whilst out in public.

I'm Grieving.

Please pass wide and slow.

I just want to find a quick way of saying 'Be gentle with me, I'm 'just' grieving.' without having to actually say it.

People don't know what to say when someone you love dies. They don't know whether to skirt around the subject or ask outright. They don't want you to be having a good day not thinking about it and then remind you with a crushing blow.

At first, it annoyed me. Of course, we haven't forgotten our loved one has died, there's a fucking great hole in the universe that they used to occupy.

But then I realised, it is a kindness, a blessing really, that people don't know what to say.

Unless they are in the club.

Even then, actually.

How do you say to someone, I am sorry that someone you loved died?

And now they are gone.

And you must navigate the world without them.

And it's a new world that doesn't make as much sense now. But it's also kind of the same for the rest of us. Everything has changed for you, whilst nothing has changed for us.

And that probably hurts. A lot.

I'm sorry about that.

God, I don't know. People want to say something, to let you know that they are thinking of you. That they know without knowing, what you are going through. Even though *they don't.* They don't know the magnitude of it, until they go through it themselves. But they know you are going through *something.*

However, when you are grieving, you can't always offer that hand to someone, to let them know that they are doing a good job of absolutely mullering their condolences to you. Because why should you?

I have found that people get really annoyed that you don't pat them on the back for making half-arsed sympathies. They are aghast when they say something that accidentally presses on the Grief Scab. Or they are so nice that it's too emotional, so you burst into loud noisy tears, and they make their excuses and go. Then you must try and explain that complexity of grief, heartache, pain and gratitude. I'm not myself, I'm grieving, I don't even know what *I* want to do or say, so how could you? I'm sorry. Please be gentle with me, even if I snap at you. I don't mean it, I'm just lost. I don't know what I need, but I know I need it. Please don't give up on me, I need you now more than ever.

But that is just too fucking much when you aren't sleeping, and you've got toothache.

So, I'd prefer to have a sign, or a hat, or a badge that says:

I'm grieving, now fuck off.

Chapter 6 – Two Letters

I have always enjoyed keeping a diary.

I've kept several over the years.

Occasionally it's been real and raw, but usually just mundane. Teenage thoughts with my crushes name written out and maths formulas of how compatible we are. *Usually not very.*

I'd furiously cross their name out and scrawl the alphabet over the top of them so no one can pry. Paranoid little soul I was. When I was introduced to the Art of Manifesting, I'd write lists, mood-boards, goals to achieve and targets to hit. I'd write stories that I'd daydreamt about, or about scenarios I wanted to happen.

I wrote at length about The Party Years, for which I would give my left tit to be able to read again now. I used to begin every entry with '*DATE : 11th Novemb 2k11*' or whatever the date was and would write lengthy passages about the politics of my friendship groups, how annoying my parents were, or being a naughty little minx.

I think I threw that diary away after a friend found *and* read it and discovered I'd shagged her boyfriend.

Outrage.

She'd skipped the part about it happening BEFORE they were together, but as she ejected my stuff from her room via the window, down to the street below, I did agree that I'd broken Girl Code and frankly my punishment should be no better than Death.

Although I would also argue that reading someone else's diary is *also* strictly forbode in Girl Code, so perhaps we are even.

But I would argue that, wouldn't I?

Speaking of death, I once wrote in an Eeyore notepad *'I wish my dad would just fucking DIE'* over and over, after a particularly savage argument with the man. Sometimes I wonder if everything I have ever manifested does come true, eventually.

Ryan and I joke that he is perpetually unlucky, whilst I seem to be consistently lucky.

If I need it to be a green light, it usually is.

Whereas when Ryan is driving, he hits red lights all the way.

I got a 'Lucky' horseshoe tattooed on my upper arm for this reason, whilst Ryan got his 'Fuck Luck' broken horseshoe on his forearm. Of course, I know that neither of us is lucky nor unluckier than the other.

Really - if I counted all the happenings in my life, I could sit and ponder why so many sad things have happened and be all maudlin and woeful about it.

I could look at Ryan with his two stable parents, and countless aunts and uncles that all adore him, and cheer him on in everything he does – and now me too. And consider him to be quite lucky.

A little bitter part of me is seething with jealousy that not only does he get longer with his dad than I do mine, but he seems intent on wasting that extra time. Not bothering to check in or trying to avoid his parents at every cost. We argue about it often. How lucky he is to have such brilliant people who just want to love him. How lucky he is to have an opportunity to learn from my misfortune and nurture his relationships before it's too late. I can see it; I can see what luck he has. But he doesn't listen, I'm not sure anyone does.

Not until it's too late.

I'm sitting with some sewing in front of me, I haven't managed any of it yet, I'd hoped getting it out would prompt me into doing something productive, but I'm so tired all the time that fetching all the ingredients I needed to begin the sewing has made me feel instantly bored of the whole idea.

'I would have quite liked something of Dad's now I think about it you know.' I call to Ryan in the other room.

'Well, you should have grabbed it then,' He calls back, helpfully. 'Hindsight...!'

I pick at my nail. Hindsight indeed. *Hindsight pisses me off.*

The letterbox chings, and two letters drop on to the floor. Ryan scoops them up, then drops them into my lap.

'Stop picking.' He scolds me, but he doesn't say it unkindly. I've developed a picking habit lately, my nails, my face, my hair. Nothing is off limits, as long it peels, plucks, or pops.

I don't even realise I'm doing it, until a bloody hole appears in my chin, or a hangnail rips off, or a chunk of hair falls to the floor. I look horrendous, blotchy red skin, stubby chewed nails. But I can't stop. It's a vice, I know, Ryan knows. But I don't drink, smoke or do drugs, so I think its fair game.

I flip the two envelopes over. The first letter looks official, I groan immediately. Dead Dad stuff. That's all I ever seem to get now.

I want to return them all to sender. Yes, I am *aware* my dear *fadder* is dead, I do not need the reminder. It sits heavy on my chest at 2am, whilst my family sleeps. It whips up memories I'd long pushed away. It curls around my time with Lily, poking in and showing me that one day I'll leave her like this. On her own. No one to talk to about it because I didn't bother giving her a sibling.

Irony is, I have a twin brother that I haven't heard from, a sister who I can't talk to and a mother who helpfully told me 'Well, I never had a dad really, so I can't really help you through this.'

I'm on my own too.

No. Ryan listens. He lets me cry and doesn't moan that his t-shirt is now soaked through. He lets me cry myself out and when I rise out of the abyss of grief to catch my breath, there's a cup of tea on the side. He doesn't try to make me feel 'OK' – whatever that is. He keeps me on track, he lets me whinge about what an utter bastard Dad was, and then flick to how amazing he was too. He understands – there were two Dads. Horrible, bastard, controlling Dad. Then kind, interesting, funny Dad.

He never ever reminds me that Dad and I weren't talking when he died.

He doesn't need to.

I push that dark thought down, I'm not ready, not ready to flay that wound. Not yet. That's the weight that sits on me in the day, the one I keep adding to, refusing to face the worst of it all. Waiting for the house to fall asleep before it winds around my body and threatens to crush me.

'Are you going to open that or are you waiting for it to fall open?' Ryan cuts through my thoughts again. He's sat next to me, ready to tackle the fall-out of whatever these two letters hold.

The other envelope is small and handwritten. It's fatter, like it's got photographs in.

I decide to open the official one first, rip that plaster off – get the boring stuff out of the way, then look through the photos of the second one to cheer myself into crying. *Grief hour has been moved forward, I console myself gleefully.*

I peel open the official letter.

It's from my aunt.

'As you know, Mark did not have an official will or testament when he died. I have been sorting through his other records and discovered he had been paying into a pension in the months before he died. As per his wishes, he has named you, Gylisa, and Tom, as his beneficiaries upon his death.

The sum of £12,500 will be split between you equally, with £2,500 going to Mum (Grandma) to reimburse for his funeral costs.

Please contact his pension provider directly, and the sum will be paid to you. If you can make payment to Grandma for the funeral, that would be appreciated. The details are included on the other side.

Regards, '

Five fucking grand.

I read it out to Ryan, and we begin to buzz with excitement.

I'll be getting five thousand pounds.

That's the most money I will have *ever* had in my bank account. A comma, finally in the plus side, instead of the negative. A gift. For me, from Dad.

We immediately chat ideas, what we should do with it. A cup of tea is made, whilst we agree how best to use such a much-needed boost. We feel like we've won the lottery.

The second letter is forgotten about until we return to the living room.

'Oh, I'm not sure I want to look at photos now, it'll just bum me out.'

Ryan thrusts the heavier envelope into my hand. 'Whatever it is, it can't be worse than five grand dropping in your lap…'

An address on the back is for a house in Cheltenham. I don't recognise it. Puzzled, I lift a card out. It isn't photographs. Just a card, a little black notebook, and an earring.

I examine the earring. A silver skull with a top hat on. It's pushed through a scrap of card with handwriting that says 'From Dirty. FEB 1986'

I turn the card over. It's a print of a Claude Monet – Waterlilies. Green Reflections.

Dear Gylisa,

Enclosed is your dear Fathers diary.

As promised to your Mum, I kept it safe until the time came to pass it on.

Included is an earring that your Dad gave to me on a very cold and snowy day in Oddington, by the old church.

He was a wonderful anarchic remedy for me after the death of my husband.

Your Dad will always be a glorious young punk to me.

Remembered and loved forever.

Love, Light and Peace.

Elizabeth.

It's Liz. Auntie Liz.

She wasn't my real auntie, of course. And I didn't remember seeing her at the funeral. A few faces hadn't been there, but then Dad's old punk friends would see a funeral as a stiff boring way to say goodbye. They would have said goodbye in their own way, I guess.

Liz had been an old girlfriend of Dads, Mum always said. We used to visit her when I was younger, and always referred to her as Auntie Liz. Her Scottish accent was still there as she clucked over us, marvelling at whatever mess we were making. She was a beautiful big-bosomed lady, and her kids had been my 'other' cousins. I thought of her fondly as I examined the little black book in my hands.

This was Dads.

The tattered book had fallen away from the spine, the edges all rough and bent. The first page fell into my lap, and I saw names and addresses of Dad's closest friends. Then in shaky handwriting –

'2017 – After I have died, could you please send this to Irving Walsh. The Great Diary Project. LONDON.'

After I have died. The questions immediately begin talking over each other in my head. *What does this mean?* Does this fraying black book hold the answers I haven't let myself consider?

I feel a rough jumper wipe my cheeks. I'm crying, again. Of course, I am.

My eyes meet Ryan's. I can't believe this.

'What were you just saying?' Ryan smiles at me, tears fill his eyes too. I shake my head, unsure what he's getting at.

'Something of your dad's. What were you just wishing for?' He offers. 'Now, you have both. Something for the future, and something from the past.'

I flick through the pages, needing more, drunk on this new connection to Dad. Where grief sat, now hope whispered, as though reading this book alone was a direct communication with him. A little part of me, not big enough to take over the excitement and glee coursing through my veins, making my hands shake as I hold this piece of my father – is looking for answers.

Answers to the Big Question.

The one I didn't want to ask, but now…it looked like I might be able to find the answer to.

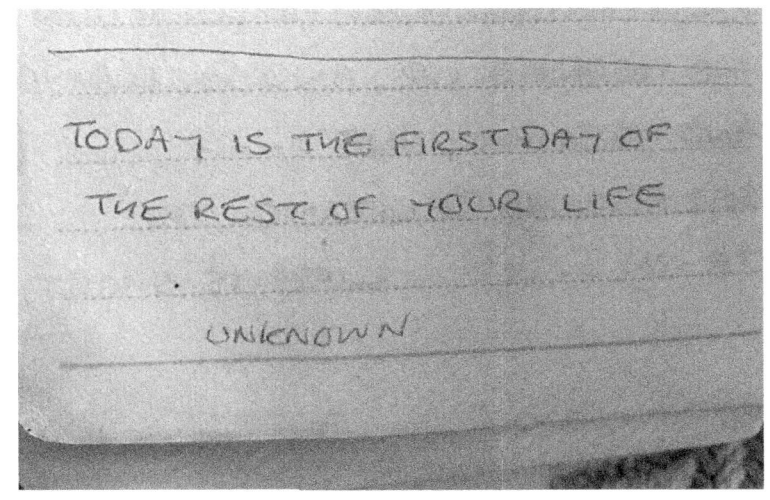

Dad's diary.

Chapter 7 – Time Travel

15 November 91.

Fuck, am I pissed OFF! Stuck on a junction type roundabout. Waiting for a lift to warmth. Over a thousand cars must have passed me today and only three gave me a ride. Now, well now I'm sitting on a sandbag, next to a lamppost and huddled in the corner of a crash barrier trying in vain to keep warm.

At least I've got the hope of a ride to warm me and these fingerless gloves I picked up before I left the s'mornin'. Soon...Soon...Those ever-faithful mates will turn up.

Hopefully before I die of exposure.

What a shitty place to sit.

Give me Julies inner thighs anytime.

Dirty.

Ps. Shit, I've just seen an ice gritter go past on the dual carriageway, no wonder I'm cold.

I'm transported there with him as I read those words. The icy wind whipping around me too, as I watch him huddle his dark coat around himself. I know exactly what he's wearing, even though he only mentioned his hideous fingerless gloves. A dark wool coat cloaks his shoulders, a paisley print cravat stuffed in the pocket, peeking out as the only bit of colour. Badges and pins glinting in the streetlights glow. His hair, dark and wild, short at the top, then tapering down into thin dreadlocks down to his chest.

The notebook rests on his thigh, as his shaky hands scribble his thoughts down.

November 1991. I'm not born yet. But I'm there with him, waiting for those ever-faithful friends, soon to be my Godparents, to scoop him up, and return him home.

I feel as though I've time travelled, as I look up and remember I'm at home. The icy scene melts away, and my living room replaces it. My home. Cornwall.

This notebook isn't just the scribblings of a mad man, although – I snigger to myself, *they definitely are.* This book has just become the most valuable non-living thing I possess.

I've been waiting for a sign from Dad.

I don't believe in ghosts, but I have been waiting or hoping for that feeling so many people talk about. A Knowing. That feeling of comfort, that your loved one is here. They've come back, to reassure you. To make sure you don't feel alone.

But I hadn't felt it.

It annoyed me, like waiting for that rush of love that everyone tells you about when Lily was born – but it never came. Everyone had assured me that moment would be life-changing, that everyone felt it, like a bolt of lightning, like a tangible shimmering ground-breaking moment. A euphoria, the moment my eyes met hers.

I distinctly remember feeling totally shortchanged after looking at my baby and thinking *'who the fuck are you?'* as this tiny, new stranger peered back up at me. I wondered then if people made it up, because they so felt that we *should* feel that way at birth, and now they were lying about having a love that transcends death too.

Maybe everyone felt so strongly that we should feel those things, they simply wished it into existence?

I didn't feel that Dad had dropped in, he hadn't sent a sign just for me. Not even reading his diary. I felt as though I was there, but in an echo of a memory. I could look, and see – but not touch, or speak. I could visualise it so clearly, and yet almost translucent too. Watching on in a memory, one I have never been privy to before the moment I read it. That's it, I think – the lump that gathers, it's that feeling of realising there are so many things I wish to talk to you about now, Dad, but I can't. All you left was your echo. A memory. Nothing else.

Worse still, I wonder to myself sadly – *did I know you at all Dad? All these things I'm only learning about you now.*

A lady contacts me to offer a tarot reading. She's heard that I've lost my dad and offers her services as a spiritualist medium. I'm not interested, but she isn't charging and is persistent– in the end I relent.

She tells me Dad is with me, because - of course she does. I ask if he's in the house, as I haven't 'felt' him. A chink in my indifferent armour. That little wisp of hope that maybe I've missed it, and he's been trying.

No, she says. He's outside, in the garden. By the chairs.

It's an immediate sore point for me, as he never came. He'd never visited me here. In my more morose confused grief, I'd cried that he wouldn't be able to find me as spirit, because he'd never had my address whilst living.

That Difficult Relationship rears its head, and I choke down the tears before they take over, again. But the thought has reached my mind, and I can't deny it. I'd lost him before I lost him.

'He's in the garden, hiding. He doesn't feel like he can come forward. He doesn't feel welcome.'

I don't reply, it's too devastating a thought.

She continues anyway. 'He's got a darkness in him, a heavy sorrow. He can't shake it…'

I hang up.

There had been no signs. Not once had a I seen a robin and thought 'that's Dad' with the unshakable confidence that so many other people I knew did. Butterflies were just that. Feathers just meant a pillow had come undone.

Nothing moved in the house inexplicably. Nothing lost appeared in front of me. Shadows didn't move in the background. A rich earthy smell never filtered through to me. I hadn't felt it when he died, and I hadn't felt him since.

Nothing.

Dad had gone.

And he wasn't coming back.

Chapter 8 – Denial, It's Not A River.

'I don't know how to say this G, but I think you'd regret not seeing him now.'

I'm at the canal boat that Mum lives on, after hearing the news Dad is in hospital. Hannah, my best mate is with me. We'd planned to walk up to my old house- Dad's old house -and peer in, see if we could conjure up any ghosts. Instead, we've got a real one on our hands.

Mum pushes me again. 'G, I know it's not easy. But you need to forget the past and see him in the now.'

She's right of course, but I am struggling to understand.

Dad's been in hospital hundreds of times before, and he's always gotten better and come home. It's just another hospital trip. Another 'incident.' I'm trying to tell her this without saying it. It's not going well. Mum is being unusually persistent.

I feel childlike in my need for things to be the same as they always have been. I feel like I'm being shoved into adult mode and want to run to my mummy and have her make it all better.

Instead, she's spun me around and shoved me on my way.

When we got to the hospital, the nurse led Hannah and me to intensive care to see him.

'He's in palliative care,' she explained. *Palliative care?* I've heard the word before, but I don't know what it means. She doesn't elaborate further, and I scowl in response. Everyone seems to be trying to communicate something deeper, something more serious, but no one seems to be actually saying it. It's beginning to piss me off. I want to scream - if you want me to act like an adult, then speak to me like one.

The nurse notices my scowl and looks to Hannah for confirmation. She doesn't give one. I look between the two of them for the missing link. It doesn't come. Why is everyone being so fucking secretive?

'It's end of life.' The nurse offers, finally. Her eyes search mine for understanding, and she must see the realisation.

Oh.

My heart feels heavy in my chest, like every beat is hard work. I feel like I might be going into the slowest shock ever. My ears are ringing, but faintly. My fingertips throb. My brain fights this news, trying to protect me. *End of life.* 'Maybe.' – my brain chimes in. 'No.' My consciousness retorts. *'End of life means dying.'*

My Dad is dying in here.

The nurse leads us in, and wittering on about how they were making him comfortable. Her eyebrows furrowed in worry, and I assume – polite sadness for us.

'You can speak to him.' She offers. 'If you want to. It's just a waiting game now.'

Her voice trails off as I take in the scene in front of me.

Where my dad was meant to be, is a shell of a man. He looked so small. This man - who could bellow across four fields in an almighty roar. Who could leer over you until you bent to his will. Who could turn a house into a hurricane. Who would scoop up our ginger moggy into his arms and purr at him. His giant hand would encase mine at the dinner table without words, just to say – 'I love you darling.' My big scary, gentle giant. *He was going to die here.* In this bed. Very soon.

So - I chatted to him and told him he would be OK, and we could talk properly when he woke up. That Parsley, our cat - was happy living on Mums boat now. That Lily was getting even bigger, he'd never believe it. She was so tall. That I'd bring her to him, and she could sit on the bed and chatter away – like toddlers do.

That I forgave him for being such a hard bastard, even if I understood it even less now that I had my own daughter. That I would never shout at her and make her tremble. That I'd always keep her safe, and guard her from the world, instead of booting her out – too young to face it alone. None of it mattered now, I told him. All that mattered was him getting better.

He squeezed my hand, and I held his whilst Hannah looked on. I left him a card that said how much I loved him, so he'd read it when he woke up.

And then he got better and came home. I tried then, having come so close to losing him. Made sure to make time to visit and invited him to my home too. And when he did, we sat in the garden, chatted about future garden plans, what I needed to dig and where. When I should prune the roses that had started curling round the fence. We drank so many cups of tea that the mugs got stained, and I'd noticed it every time I reached for one in the cupboard.

He lived, and life continued as it was, but slightly better, because we'd come so close to the end – it had made us realise what we stood to lose.

Only, that's not what happened.

This would be a fucking short book if it had.

I wish, I wish so much I could rewrite history, that things had gone the way I see they should have now, but that's not how life is, not really.

I'd shuffled in, saw this shell of a man, a stranger in that bed, pretending to be my dad.

And realised *I was too late.*

Shock of what I saw before me took over my whole body, and I just choked. My brain was fighting so much to find the lie, to find anything it could cling to, to prove that what I was seeing was fake, false, an untruth. *But it couldn't.*

I would have turned and bolted out the door, but Hannah was blocking my escape route. She would follow me if I did cut and run, she would just know to. I knew that. But right now, she was urging me forward. It seemed everyone could see and understand the gravity of this situation before I did.

'Why don't you say something Gee?' Hannah nudged me gently.

But I couldn't.

My mouth kept opening and shutting but nothing would come out. As though my voice box had been yanked out of my throat without me realising. My eyes skirted around the room as questions flew through my mind.

How did you end up here?

Are you going to be OK?

Can you hear us?

Have you gone...already?

Do you know I'm here?

Would you want me here?

All those and a million more flew through my mind, whilst equally the inanest rubbish too. My brain was desperately trying to protect me from the hurt about to flood in and distracted me with the view from the dark window, looking around curiously at the state of the other poor souls in the ICU. To see if they were real too. To see, to hope they were all faking it. For some long-winded drawn-out horrible joke at my expense.

I took in his table, and the glasses and jug of water. My gaze lingered on the ring of water left by someone else's vacant cup, and I wondered who had sat here before me. The smell was a mixture of hospital, illness and breath. I thought about how warm it was in there. I stared at the fluorescent lighting, until it burned black dots into my retinas. I wanted to find something to wipe down, to rearrange or tidy. My eyes landed on the blanket at the foot of his bed, and immediately I was cast back to our baby blankets as kids-

No. I forced myself into the present, Mum's words ringing in my ears.

In the absence of words, I held his hand and gave it a soft squeeze.

I'm here Daddy.

I love you.

I am so confused; this feels so grown up and scary and strange. Almost dreamlike. That's my *dad* lying there, my daddy. One of my pillars. The reason that I am here at all. My hero, as a child, my aggressor as a young woman. I love him so deeply, and yet I don't like him much at all.

No, I do – I think, as hot tears spill over. *I do love you, Dad.*

I can't bear to think anything negative in case it curses him into death. I'm trying to scratch that word out of my vocabulary at all, willing it away. My OCD brain is running wild, taunting me with intrusive thoughts. *If you think about death, you've killed him.* I force myself back into the positive. Willing away any and all bad memories, certain that if one slips through, I'll be condemning him before his time.

I force myself back on track. *I hope you are proud of us, Dad. All of us, not just me.* I think it, but I can't say a word. Nothing will come out. I'm still opening and closing my mouth, goldfish-like, whilst holding his warm, swollen hand.

I think back to holding his arm during dinner, just gazing at him – full of the most innocent love. Then to returning home to my room trashed, my prized belongings strewn across the driveway.

He wasn't well, was he? My inner voices are battling with each other so fiercely, I'm not sure which one to listen to. My whole brain feels a mess, as I examine Dad's face for some element of him in there. He looks so unfamiliar. I try to place it. He looks older, his grey hair hanging limply. He's lost weight too.

Then I realise, why he looks so different. I've seen it before, but only ever glimpses. *He looks vulnerable.* My big, strong, scary Daddy is weak and dying. And I can't bear to be confronted with it.

I squeeze his hand again, hoping, wishing for a response. Something that would prove the nurses wrong. Prove Mum wrong. Everything could go back to how it was, we could all say how sorry we were that it had come to this, and how much we loved each other. We'd all just gotten a bit lost.

But no return squeeze came.

I looked over his face, the laughter lines faded. His frown melted away. My daddy was gone. He was still alive, but not on his terms. He'd hate this. He wouldn't bear any of us seeing him like this.

I feel disgusted with myself for looking at him. I turn away out of respect, face Hannah and see her eyes filling with tears. *Oh.*

'Are you OK?' I ask her, finally, words bless my mouth again.

'Well, no, Gee.' She shrugged, speaking softly. 'I've known him a long time…you know-.' She trailed off.

Of course, he'd been part of her life too.

For years and years, and she'd seen it all. She'd laughed with him in the good times, sheltered me in the bad. She'd taken me under her wing and never asked questions about why I didn't want to go home, she'd just set another place at the table or walked with me for hours in the cold around the village. She understood that it was a complicated thing, and that was OK. She was just here, no questions asked. And she was here now too. For the first time I realised she had always been there. My anchor in every storm.

She knew. She knew this was it, and it was time for me to realise it too.

I was going to walk out of that door, and never see my Dad ever again. The book would shut. The door locked. He would stay there, and I would be here. Then he would be gone.

I squeezed her arm. Sad that she was sad, for him and for me. A tearful smile came back. *She knew.*

I wrote him a card, still refusing to release the glimmer of hope that he'd return. *There is always hope.* It's tattooed on both mine and Hannahs wrists, my 18th birthday present. I'd drawn it for us, and we'd chanted it back to each other.

There is always hope.

If I write him a card, he'll have to come back and wake up – to read it.

I turned to Hannah, who gave me a 'well-done' smile. My dear best friend, I was so glad she was here.

'I don't want to be inappropriate Gee, because I know this is your dad and everything, but your eyes are like, so electric blue right now.'

She was gazing at me, giving me the strangest of compliments. A beautiful sad girl. I gave her a watery smile, as tears hit my eyelashes and slid down my cheek.

'Well, I don't want to be inappropriate either, but I really need a poo.'

At that admission, we burst into laughter, a remedy for the heaviness of the situation. Realising where we were – Intensive Care – not the place for laughing, despite the turn of phrase that it's the best medicine – perhaps not for this sad lot. We quickly went quiet, but it was too late. We had to rush out of the ward, me comically holding onto my arse to try and force Hannah to break the silence with more laughter. That giddy giggly feeling of laughing with your best mate replacing the impending grief as we skidded down the corridor in search of the loos.

It reminded me of another memory, I hadn't thought about it for years. As kids, Hannah and I were usually exploring, or getting ourselves into mischief. We were a nosy pair of tomboys, often climbing something or breaking something, or trying to discover something new. We knew the village like the back of our hands, and as such, we were larking around when we found ourselves at the village church, *wild – I know.*

Bored, we were throwing pinecones or whatever it was to amuse ourselves, when we came across a young woman crying at the foot of an elm tree.

We immediately rushed over to check if she was OK, but of course she wasn't. Great, heavy sobs fell out of her, and she clung to us, as we desperately tried to find out what the matter was. The devilish streak in me was delighted at the thought of a mystery we may have to uncover. Eventually she managed to burst out with - 'I've lost him, my brother!'

'Oh, well where did you lose him?' Hannah had responded with, the penny not dropping for her that this poor girl's brother had been lost somewhere he couldn't be found. I'd have kicked her if she'd been in reach, but both of us were around the girl's shoulders, rubbing them in a way we hoped was bringing some comfort. I was trying to have a silent conversation above her head with Hannah, raising my eyebrows in a 'lost-in-this-instance-means-he-is-probably-dead' manner, to which Hannah was shrugging back. I'd begun rubbing her jumper off her shoulder and was now just making her porcelain pale skin rash red. I then noticed and gently patted it back into place.

'No….no…just now. He's died.' She wailed the last word, almost throwing herself onto the floor, prompting more back rubs and strokes from me. I threw in a few 'Shush, shush..' noises for effect.

'Oh, gosh, I'm so sorry…' Hannah began to say, trying to catch my eye. I was avoiding her gaze at this point, as the gravity of the situation was such that I knew if we had eye contact the pair of us, the little ghouls we were, would burst into laughter. Not because we thought it was funny that this poor girl's brother had died, obviously, but precisely *because* the situation was so serious and not funny, that bursting into laughter would be the most awful thing to do.

The taboo of it so naughty, that I knew if I so much as saw Hannah's lips curve upwards, I would be rendered completely hysterical.

We managed to rein it in and comforted this poor bereaved girl as best we could, even making her laugh.

'He was ill, so it was expected,' Abi – as we'd found out she was called – explained. 'But at the same time, him actually going was just so UNEXPECTED.'

'What happened?' Hannah asked earnestly.

Abbi tried to explain, he'd had cancer. They'd all been around his bedside. It wasn't certain if it had happened just now, or a week ago. But we listened intently anyway. Her voice had stopped cracking now and was almost sing-song instead.

'And he was there, all wrapped up in his juvet…'

At this point, we had done so well, each of us avoiding the others gaze, and making sure to keep absolutely transfixed on Abi's words. Holding it together well. It wasn't funny, of course it wasn't. Neither of us would have said that it was funny. Her brother had died, it was a terrible, tragic thing. It was harrowing, watching her world crumble in front of us.

But this was the fizzing point, the vinegar stroke of the conversation and she'd sent us into full climax by pronouncing the word 'duvet' wrong.

We erupted into laughter, and the lid came totally off. And Abi laughed with us, the way you do when someone is in hysterics at a joke you haven't heard – it's so contagious, you can't help but join in.

She was so unbelievably sweet, this little Betty Boop character – a tiny ditsy blonde being funny without realising – so that was what we quickly went with, Hannah quickly patching up the conversation with a little white lie, I forget what she said, I'd been too busy willing my face into seriousness again. We all laughed together, thankful at the release.

We then walked her home and gave her Hannahs phone number, so if she ever needed a chat we could be there.

I kicked Hannah up the arse on the way home and said if Abi ever did come back, we were under strict instructions not to piss ourselves laughing at the word 'juvet'.

'But she said it with such CONVICTION!'

I retell the story to Hannah now as we leave the toilets and find our way back through the maze of corridors. She's laughing away and remembering out loud her side of it all.

Her words fade away as I think about Dad in one of those beds upstairs.

This isn't really goodbye, is it Dad?

I love you.

11 Dec 91.

Sitting in the Vic Bus station in Nottingham. This morning I received a letter, not much strange about that. Only this letter was going to change my life.

I'm pregnant.

Funny how you can feel happy, even ecstatic, but at the same time a sense of guilt – not really apprehension – definitely guilt. I've just changed someones life totally. After all, I cannot marry Julie and even the thought of moving back down to Chelty fills me with dread.

But if I'm really gonna be a Dad I want to help my off-spring. Fill him/her with love and knowledge. But from 100 miles away that's impossible.

Well I did use to think I had an answer for almost every problem but this one I'm totally confused.

I love Julie, but to live with or near her, I would totally in my own selfish way destroy what she did have for me. Even if she does think I'm wonderful now I seriously doubt it. Being near me would certainly change that.

But then again – I'm a DAD! I'm a DAD! I'm a DAD!

Oinkykerfuckingploinkee!!!

At Birmingham Shit Station -

I'm still goin' to be a father although the more I think about it, not a very good one.

I get the feeling that the only thing I'm gonna be around for is the conception. What can I do about it? Well money for a start. Why does everything always boil down to money.

You know, I wonder what she'll look like? Julie and the child?

This will create a big difference in our relationship.

RESPONSIBILITIES.

13th December 1991 (Friday)

I've slowed down as it's sunk in, I managed not to burst out telling Hans etc.
But only just. I still love it! What a beauty! Me, I'm gonna be a Dad. A part time Dad but a Dad nonetheless. Life will never quite look the same again.

For the good?

It's now 1am(ish) I'm sitting in Moreton in my old bedroom, I'm pissed off, I want to be in Shurdy, I want to be with Julie!

Sitting here everything seems completely irrelevant, my mind is racing along about thoughts of what life will be like as a Dad.

True, once reality has happened things will be/seem different but now…I love it!

I want to write a new will with all my possessions, mainly my records to go to my first live child, and a letter explaining that even though I might not have been there everyday, I still loved him/her and this music will help them realise why. Sitting downstairs earlier I was dying to tell the folks that I was going to make them grandparents but I just can't, well not yet anyway!

Life will be so different now!

And that whole new learning experience will be such a rush. I'm going to love it no matter what happens.

Winks in his Wide Boy attitude mode is right! About me feeling guilty about not being there!

I remember not congratulating Paul on the announcement of his fatherhood because he would only be a part time Dad. But why create a situation with Julie that will end up with us hating each other? Which I know WILL happen if I was to live with her in my want to help her bring our child up! And believe me I WANT to bring our child up! I hope maybe my absence will help, the trouble is I can't find this out now, only in 20 years time.

Which of course means staying alive, although I always went for the chance of burning myself to death in a few years time.

Now, I want to live long and hard to watch my child become an intelligent human with the ability to help and love the human race in years to come.

And for them to know that I was their Dad and everything I know is within them! A hippie concept maybe but if I can't change the planets self-destruction, then maybe my children can?

Anyway – I'm gonna be a DAD! It's really going to happen! Oh Wow!

Ps. Give up the smoking (Julie).

Chapter 9 – D-Day

Dad died.

His card, that I'd sworn he would wake up to read. That was private. Just for him. A part of me had thought, should he go – it goes with him.

Mum had opened it. 'To read to him.'

It had vexed me; I knew that wasn't the reason at all.

My sister and Mum would have seen the card, and the big red button it represented and wouldn't have been able to help themselves but pry. A diary that has been left out, a room left unlocked.

I knew this, when I wrote it. So- no grand gesture of secrecy lay within in. No lengthy essay.

It simply said:

Dad,

I love you,

I just wanted you to know, I was here.

Thank you, for everything.

Gylisa x'

Five days after I had left the hospital, the phone call had come. He'd gone.

Mum said that someone had been there with him when he went, and she had asked that a window be opened after he passed. A gust of wind had blown in, swirled round the room, and disappeared again.

Mum didn't need to say it, but we both felt his presence, his soul, had gone with that gust.

'The body is just the shell, Gee.' She told me. I believed her.

Where had he gone? That was my next question. It's the Big Question isn't it?

How can someone be here one minute, but gone the next?

We weren't a religious family. I was brought up to be staunchly non-Christian, although being a tearaway teenager in my household had meant I'd started following Christianity to rebel.

I'd found comfort in having a bible under my pillow. I'd sought refuge at churches. I'd prayed and tried to speak with God.

I don't know if he was just busy or not answering, but I'd never felt a connection come back to me. My questions had always been left unanswered. I craved that faraway look that Christians got when they talked about their belief. How they were staunch in their teachings, how they felt comfort knowing they'd go to Heaven. I just couldn't dial in.

I'd always felt there was something more, something else out there. After a particularly nasty fight with Dad, I'd run over the fields to the church only to find it locked shut.

As rain clouds had descended, I'd sat in the churchyard, the same spot that Abi had found years before and cried. Hoping for a Good Samaritan to find me, even if they just laughed at me for mispronouncing something and fucked off again.

No one came. I'd prayed and asked for a sign from God, but all I'd got was a smack from Dad when I returned for 'disappearing'. God couldn't answer my prayer 'Why do bad things happen to innocent people?' and so my flickering faith washed away with the rain.

I'd also found what I believed to be several loopholes within Christianity, the main one being – if I prayed for forgiveness then I'd still get into Heaven, which kind of negated the whole *'being good for life gives you the golden ticket'.*

I had tried, as a child to be 'good' always, and Mum and I have theorized whether that was the real trigger for my obsessive compulsions. 'If I think something 'bad'- bad things will happen.'

It had been confirmed by thinking about poor Scott dying, and then he did. I'd caused it and couldn't tell anyone. I was a mind-murderer and would have to repent for the rest of my life to make up for it.

By the time I reached 20 years old, I'd done so many dreadful things I felt that if I got to the pearly gates and St Peter showed them to me to ask if I was remorseful and wanting to repent – seeing them all played back to back like a You've Been Framed compilation would crack me right up, and I'd still be laughing all the way down as he opened the cloud trapdoor and damned me to fall to Hell.

In short – Christianity was not for me.

Dad had believed in Buddhism and had taught us as children about karma and enlightenment. Believing that we needed to find happiness within ourselves, rather than what we achieved or owned. Occasionally I'd imagined him reincarnated as an earwig when he was pissing me off, which amused me greatly.

When asking Mum or Dad what they wanted me to be when I 'grew up' they had both annoyingly replied 'happy.' Which was a real shitter when I was trying to choose what to do for my A Levels.

What was I supposed to do with that? At least if they'd have said 'we want you to become a lawyer', I could follow a set-out pathway to achieve it.

Instead, I felt as though if I didn't achieve happiness, I'd not only be fucking miserable, but I'd have the guilt of letting my parents down too. *Thanks.*

I smirk down at my chest now, thinking about it as I sit with my thoughts once more. It's all I have done since the phone call. Since the funeral. Since the 'After' had begun. Sit and reminisce. My mind floats from one memory to the next, as though I'm trying to refresh them all. I tell myself if I go over them it'll bring me closer to Dad. One memory may hold the key and open the gate to enlightenment.

The final stage. Enlightenment in Grief Speak is acceptance.

Accepting that your loved one has gone somewhere they can't be reached.

Until then I must go over and over the karmic cycle until something slots into place and I can get the answers to the questions that plague the night.

Why?

Why?

Why?

Comfort only comes in Grief Hour. Sometimes not even then, but at least I've found an outlet for the rip-roaring emotion that needs to flood out of me unannounced. I've spent the last week crying at the drop of a hat. 'Oh….' Ill groan. *'Dad wore a hat once…'* And then I'm started off again.

Honestly, I'm starting to do my own head in, never mind anyone else's.

12 Dec 91.

OH WOW!!!!

It would appear that it's all true, I'm gonna become a DAD! A thousand thoughts a second seem to be passing through my brain.

It's a girl? It's a boy? Name? What do he/her look like? I'm a Dad! What will the folks say? I'm a Dad! It's a girl? Colour of her hair? Can I play music to him/her before they're born? I'm a Dad! What will the Folks say?

Over and over, it's great – what a wonderful high, I've helped create. I'm stuck – my mind just won't accept the hard work that this will entail. Although for me – only having to be around again..!

Although not all the time which makes me feel guilty but I will love her/him forever. It's just totally fulfilling to know that I'm the cause for the creation happening in Julie! I'm a Dad! I'm a Dad! I'm a Dad! I'm a Dad! What the fucking hell are the folks going to say! Oh a Bum Thought came in there – I'm a DAD! I'm a Dad!

Still the 12th… Midnightish.

Well what would I say, what a couple of days. Even with all the smoke I've put away I feel so unbelievably HAPPY! To start with, just the thought that I'm a Dad! And she's carrying my baby – gives me a ragin stiffy!

Well, I drifted about all day, eventually getting my stuff together and catching the bus for Moreton.

Got in late, and first bumped into Max! Very weird! Over to the phonebox to get Winks and an hour later we're parked and skinning up! Talking!

So good to get it all off my chest only to be confronted with a problem of Winks. It seemed totally irrelevant to him. Actually, more like shock.

Did go down to the pub later, found Bri, Blob and Shaggy! Good chat, good laugh – but it all seemed so pointless in comparison to the birth of my child!!!!

I did manage to not tell 'em so I can drop the bomb to the bastards on crimbo day!

Let em take the piss out of me until their blue in the face, I don't care it all feels so right! I've got to pass out tomorrow and see how I feel. Now though, I love it! What a high!

Chapter 10 - Paradoxes

Reading Dad's diary, again.

It's so strange to hear his thoughts and feelings about me, and my brother – although at this point, he didn't know he was getting a BOGOF offer yet. Imagine that, getting your head around becoming a 'new person', this 'father' 'dad' 'parent' figure, only to have two kids to shape and mould at once. A true Baptism of Fire. An heir and a spare. At least if you fuck one up you've got the other to fall back on. A draft and a final piece. His excitement and joy at the prospect of us is so tangible, and yet – I know how the story goes.

I've avoided all things Christmas this year. I don't want Christmas Future to happen, I want the poached egg ghost from the Muppets Christmas Carol to send me back to Christmas Past. It feels so strange to be learning this – the start of my story, at the end of his. Strange isn't the word perhaps. Totally unfair.

I wish I'd asked him about it when he was here, it feels like such an opportunity missed. Then again, would he have been honest? Are we ever honest with our loved ones, or do we give them a watered down more palatable version, to save their feelings?

In diary form, we can speak to whoever we choose, say whatever we want.

Reading his words, knowing he believed – when writing them – that no one would ever read it. It was just for him.

His thoughts, his fears, his excitement.

My version of Dad had always been steadfast, a man's man who knew his own mind and didn't care what anyone thought. As Auntie Liz said – a glorious young punk.

But now I see him for what he truly was. Nervous, afraid. Excited but full of doubt. Doubting himself but wanting to do his best. Not sure what his full potential was. Maybe even a little scared to find out, should his full potential fall short of what he believed, or hoped it was.

It was revealing parts of him that I share, that I had no idea about at all. He was just a young guy, with no clue. Just like I feel now, his female counterpart. I suppose I am him, a part of him. When you are a kid, adults seem so…wizened and old. Like raisins to grapes.

But he was young, in his twenties. Just like me, now.

I think back to being a teenager, and him being just forty. I should have told him to shut up way more…what would he have done really? The thought amuses me, I did tell him to shut up, among other things.

I would say I was a royal pain in his arse, most of the time. No wonder he used to get so irritated, when I'm forty, I won't have the slightest clue how to deal with Lily if she gives me the sort of lip I gave Dad.

I used to wait for him to really go off on one and sit staring at his head. Then, whilst he was mid-sentence, I'd hold my hand up and pinch the air, squinting so the perspective meant his head filled the space between my fingers. He'd lose track of what he was saying 'What are you doing?' before realising and yelling 'Stop squeezing my fucking head!' But it was too late, the trouble I was in was rendered obsolete, I'd made him laugh. One-nil to me.

The Christmas lights on the tree fade out and pull my attention away, as I'm soaked in brief darkness before they light up again. I've spent another evening lost in fading memories. Unpeeling Dad's layers like an onion, tears and all.

Christmas, then New Years…Then this year will end, and leave him in it.

The thought pains me, I want to stop time flying past. I want to halt everything, bring it all to a standstill. I'm not ready to let him go, to leave him behind, stuck forever in this year, his final one.

I want to revisit everything, look at it all with the sort of appreciation you only get when you realise how finite it was. I hate myself for not asking these questions earlier, for not peeling back his oniony skin whilst I could still ask him – what does this mean? Or have you ever thought about that?

I want to lean on his arm whilst he's talking at the dinner table, I want to listen to his stories. I even want to pinch his stupid head.

I need to look back, I need to know him, and reading his diary so far has only made me realise, for the first time, how little I really did know him. How had this man been my father for so many years and yet I'd never sat down and got to know him?

The questions begin to rise with that oh-so-familiar lump in my throat, so many more questions now and I'll never be able to ask him.

That option has gone.

The worst feeling of grief is all the halves. Half memories, half jokes. Half questions that only one man can answer fully. But he's gone and taken all that with him.

I stare down at his diary on my lap. He's left something for me. Maybe, I'll find something in his past. Something that I can take to the future.

I flick through, asking, willing for him to offer some of his wisdom to me now, to show me - how to push forward – when it means leaving you behind?

How do I look ahead, knowing you are only going to get further away?

I shut my eyes and allow the next wave to hit me, I want to feel it, the way I do when I'm being tattooed. I don't fight it, but allow the pain to wash into my bones, accepting each fresh sting on my tender skin. I hear the familiar sound of paws padding along the carpet. Oh good, Bhuna my therapy cat has settled in for a late-night Grief Hour cuddle. She always knows when I need her.

Eyes still closed, I begin to press the thoughts of Dad, to find an answer to my questions, any question. Just something. A sign, Dad?

Send me something.

Anything.

At that moment, a furry thud lands on his diary, and I look down to see the cat has dropped a dead mouse in my lap.

New Years Eve '91

Well, even though I am depressed as usual. Walking into town has done some good.

I'm sitting in the square in Notts. Half a bottle and a few infills down. Theres about 2 or 3 hundred people around all waiting for the chime of midnight. It's a bit dodgy as mainly their wideboys. A very good atmosphere nonetheless. Half past 11 has just struck and caused a small celebration.

What I don't get is peoples need to celebrate the passing of time, to me it's very depressing that the year has ended and a whole new uncertain year is to begin.

Well, now (2:08am) the square has filled up to over a thousand pissheads all out for fun. I met a couple who gave me a beer to celebrate with and we got on a treat. What a laugh, all those people and that…It was wild! Even though I went down with a depression, I came out with very high spirits.

Getting home, I called in on the Doc and Missus who helped me get even more pissed and happy. I enjoyed myself.

Quote – First thing this guy said to me this year. 'Keep it up, we need people like you.'

We do, Dad.

My eyes blur as I re-read that last line.

We do. I repeat it over. I want to write it in there, next to his scrawling handwriting. I need you Dad, and you've gone and bloody *died*. I feel a wisp of Grief Anger lipping in my chest. I wish he was sat next to me just so I could call him a cunt. *'What did you do that for?'* I'd ask him. Anger is replaced by an urge to giggle, a smile creeping in the corner of my lips. *You silly dead cunt.*

It's such a paradox, I love and miss him more than I could ever find words for, suddenly I remember what I had. What the world had. A great man. An interesting individual who wasn't scared to be himself. That's what the world needs.

Instead, the world chewed him up and spat him out. So, he thought *'fuck this'* and went and died, instead of fighting to live.

Mostly, I realise as the rage-giggles simmer down again, my mind plucks out the true reason I am so angry.

I'm angry with myself.

How can I remember what I had now it's gone?

Why has this fucking diary come to haunt me?

I wonder if perhaps this is the sign from Dad after all, his ghostly hand mimicking Liz's to send his final words via letter.

Maybe my penance is to relearn all that I loved about the man, just to get to the end and lose him again. That would be such a typical thing of Dad to do, even from another realm. He always preferred a physical lesson, to a verbal one. He'd say, 'Find out how it *feels*, and you'll learn.'

What is it in fathers that make them need to be so fucking *right* all the time? I make a mental note to ask Ryan.

Will he do this to Lily? Teach her life lessons in the same way?

I do hope not. If he doesn't see her out into adulthood, I shall kill him myself. This is a dreadful lesson to teach your kids. Let us grieve an old relative instead. *Stay alive, you owe it to us.*

I see so many similarities between the two men. Both stubborn Geminis. Both interesting, incredible people, but equally difficult and annoying. Both always pushing me to be a better person, but never using that drive on themselves. As though they weren't worth it.

They both see so much potential in other people, and yet don't seem to see their own.

We'd hoped we might have twins, another Gemini father meaning it was written in the stars. But no. No BOGOF offer for us. Lily blessed us enough for two instead.

It's painful for me now, to have so many parenting questions I'll never be able to ask him. To want to show him how much I love being a parent. How amazing it is. How baffling too. How it redirected my perspective on him since becoming one.

I want him to see me being an adult, to see my impact on the world, to see if it was what he'd hoped for. *I've saved people, Dad. Good ones too. People that needed saving.*

I close my eyes tightly. *I wish you could see me, Dad. I hope I've made you proud.* Each wish sends a fresh stab of grief ache through me.

I know that when I'm done, when I reach that impossible summit of Acceptance – I'll be a better person for it.

But God, I wish I didn't have to.

24th March 1992

Well here I sit, just back from Jimi's after Geeza turned up earlier. Yes, I'm stoned.

But what has happened in the last few weeks is totally wonderful. On the last trip down south, Julie told me – we're going to have twins. What a mind-blower.

And now life is totally FANDABBYFUCKINDOZEE! We're going to live together. And hopefully start, bring up a pair of lives. I'm so in love with Julie, the idea, the twins, the whole thought of having a family, with Julie, Clair and the twins….

Having gotten some photos developed recently (of Julie) I can't help myself looking at her and…I love it!!! Mind you I'm still wasted.

Crap.

Everyday for weeks I've been waiting for the day to move and start.

I got a letter from Clair a few weeks ago, what a great feeling. I know we'll get on because I love her and she loves me. Mind you, we're bound to get on. Afterall we are both stubborn as fuck! I know with this love we will always get on (Julie and I)

You know the only bum thing that I know of is Winks has gone abroad without saying cheerio. Apparently he's got a 12 month work permit, and if he's gone that long well, he won't see our children and I can't make him Godfather.

Not only that, I posted a letter to the bum two days ago and he'd already gone.

Love Light and Peace

Dirty.

28th March 92. (?) Saturday Morning. 5.52am.

Why do I even bother trying to sleep these days! Well this time I've given up trying. It's all coming together. I'm gonna move out on Wednesday (April 1st) and all these thoughts won't leave me alone. Mind you, they're not all bad. Infact, they are mainly great, like playing strip chess with Julie, going shopping with Clair, getting a part-time job, going to register the birth(s) of our children, chasing Ju around Lecky' Hill midsummer with next to fuck all on, or – the last one before I stop to write this – going to catch a bus with Clair and introducing her as my daughter…

Now I couldn't say I'm totally happy as there are as usual as few doubts and worries in my mind, well – like I have a huge feeling that 'The Bums' will just ignore me even though I'm moving back toward some of them…actually that looks as crap as it sounds now.

And what if Julies changed her mind after all with all this stuff of mine moving in on her.

Well…

Love, Light and Peace.

Dirty.

Chapter 11 – Ch-Ch-Changes

A flash of light blinds me, and for a moment I'm seeing spots instead of faces in front of me. I blink it away, as my new dentist tells me she'll have to take the traditional impressions instead of scanning my teeth for my new Invisalign retainers. She's just taken another set of X-rays, and I wonder if my teeth are possibly the worst she's ever seen.

'So, can I have Invisalign then?' I ask her, waiting for the inevitable – '*Sorry, your teeth are past help. They really are quite dreadful. These X-Rays are actually for research so we can enter them for the World Record – Worlds Worst Teeth, Ever.*' That's what I've been telling myself she'll say the moment she looks inside my mouth.

'Oh yes!' She retorts instead. 'You're a great candidate.'

Her chipper reply lets in a sneaky bit of excitement into my heart, *wait, bloody hold up – what's this*? I almost don't know what to do with it, but helpfully I start welling up instead. I've not quite got a lid on the ol' emotions yet. I desperately try to blink away tears, my voice not working again as the dreaded lump forms in my throat, and all I can do is nod in response.

Her eyes don't miss much, and she looks at me earnestly, before choosing to ignore it, pushing on with treatment planning.

That's right, I'm using my Dead Dad Money to put a literal smile on my face, until the real one appears again.

It's the sort of irony I feel he would have appreciated.

As New Years concluded and a fresh new year rolled around without my express permission, I figured Life was going to carry on, with or without me. The sneaky little bugger.

I went to bed on January 1st, 2019. A new year. I then got up, later that day – and realised, I couldn't mope forever. My Grief Plan had always had a forward arrow, so I wanted to plod on. Phase One of learning to live with grief – figure out how to smile again.

Dad had given me more than just money, I didn't want to just fritter it away. *Well, maybe a cheeky little fritter.* But most of it would go on this, and I felt it was a worthy cause. It was Dad's last chance to give me something I wanted, and I wanted this more than anything in the whole world.

I might not feel like smiling now, but as my dentist began explaining that it would take around twenty weeks of treatment for me to see the finished result, a quiet part of me wondered if I'd be ready then.

An even quieter part of me whispered, I think so.

25th April 94.

Do people change? Are we the same person destined to follow a course?

'The caterpillar becomes the butterfly.'

Which am I? The caterpillar – the early years, The butterfly the mature (???) years.

But the caterpillar and the butterfly are both beautiful with bad ways. Is one more beautiful than the other?

So why do I feel so much more fulfilled, more expanded?

More better!?!

Do people change? I stare at Dads scrawl, a snippet of his diary written in a hurry. I wondered what he'd seen or thought of that had prompted him to quickly scribble this stream of consciousness down.

Had he felt that he'd changed? I found that hard to believe.

He'd been a miserable old bugger, and then he'd carked it.

Didn't even bother getting to the end - I mean how miserable is that?

Life is moving forward, no matter how much I wish it wouldn't, and yet I'm still awake at this hour full of questions that I am not sure I'll ever find the answers to.

A creeping feeling finds its way up my spine, and I shiver it back down. I want to shake it off, brush it away and hide in this limbo-land indefinitely.

A separate, and apparently – a much braver part of me – clings to the feeling, a curious and defiant part wants to look at it and ask why? *Why do I feel so scared to find out the answers?*

I sit and ponder, picking at another dry piece of skin on my nail, before ripping it too far and drawing blood. Ouch.

Maybe…maybe it's because I'm not sure I'll like what I see.

Chapter 12 – The Boat

Summer has slinked around on us, and it's Dad's birthday.

21st June, Summer Solstice.

It's also Father's Day, which I have been dreading. I thought I'd be almost glad it was a special offer of heartache, a two-in-one, a double whammy, *two birds, one stone.*

Now it's here though, and it feels like I've missed the bottom step of a set of stairs I thought I had imprinted on my brain. My stomach turns as I search for the safety of the floor.

We travel back up to the Cotswolds, which is the first time since the funeral. It all feels so different now. Instead of happy memories, every field, every tree and every road just led me to thoughts of Dad.

I watched fields and trees whizz past us as Ryan drives us up the motorway, and think wanly, I'd been right – Dad was our glue, and without him we have all become strangers.

Mum, my sister, Grandma and my aunt had got together to take Dad's ashes to Broadway Tower. During his wake, it had occurred to me that Dad had loved it there – his last job before we went to Yorkshire. It had seemed like the perfect place to let him watch eternity, high on the hill – views for miles.

The idea had spilled out, in my desperation to keep us all together for something, to put a contingency in place, so we wouldn't lose each other too.

Now, we'd all become so fractured, my invite had been lost in the post. My brother didn't go either - he simply hadn't been ready. I wondered how he was getting on today. I should reach out, I think.

I should.

But I can't.

Something keeps me from doing it. I don't want to peer in at his grief. I don't want to compare. Most of all, I don't want to look and see something I wished I hadn't. I didn't want to see him struggling, I didn't feel brave enough to offer a hand of comfort.

I didn't know how to yet.

I want to be upset with them for stealing my idea and doing it without me. But I can hear Toms voice now, telling me it doesn't matter. That I could go anywhere I wanted to remember Dad. That his ashes were just that – Dead Dad Dust.

It didn't matter who held it as it floated away.

It wasn't like losing Dad all over again. *It wasn't.*

Broadway Tower had been one of Dads favourite jobs, and I knew he'd been happiest there. We'd only left to move to North Yorkshire, with hopes of a better future. It had been great to start with, in a tied barn conversion and Dad's employers had been amazing. They'd invite me over for afternoon tea, as I was the only one of the three of us children who knew how to behave in front of posh folks, and they'd coo over me as I ate finger sandwiches that I thought were rancid, with a polite smile on my face.

Then they'd wanted to sell up, and all our future hopes had been dashed. We had to move, although they'd offered to buy us a home in the nearby town – Dad's pride had got the better of him and we'd taken a chance elsewhere. After that, the wheels came off – Dad's mental health had never really recovered, and well…

I wondered if he associated Broadway Tower with his last happy place, if it *was* where he should be, etched forever in the countryside.

I wanted to go back, back to the wake, back to the Hospital, back to living here, in the Cotswolds. If I could just turn back the clock, make some different choices – this could all have turned out so differently.

I'd bumped into one of my most wonderful friends, Holly, in Chipping Campden, and told her about my half-hearted plan for Dad's birthday. She'd pressed a handtied posy of flowers into my hand and told me I'd know what to do with them.

And I did.

Ryan, Lily and I went on a pilgrimage that I never thought I would walk again. I'd shown Dad this hidden gem a decade or longer ago, and my brother had told me it had been Dad's favourite. Long after I moved out, he still came up here. He'd called it 'The Boat.'

I'd never known.

There is an old tree stump, sticking out of the hill beneath Kiftsgate Gardens, and it had become so old and worn, that it looked like a boats hull stuck halfway in the earth. You could climb in and look out at the valley ahead of you, on a clear day you could see for miles.

It had been a cracking find when I came across it, and I'd half dragged Dad and Tom with me to see it one summers evening – a lifetime ago. They'd marvelled at it, but I'd had no inkling that they'd returned.

I may not have Dad with me, but if he was going to be anywhere today, I thought this might be it.

As we walked up, Ryan and Lily chattering away, my mind wandered to thoughts of Dad, that he should be here – 53 years old today, and yet he wasn't.

Once we reached the hull, I stepped into the tree and looked down the valley. Each field and tree, every curve of the landscape beyond. The houses dotted in-between. Different crops making a patchwork blanket beneath us. I took it all in, then carefully placed the posy down.

As I looked out again, a buzzard came soaring over, close enough that I could see each fleck of dark brown underneath its chest. It caught my eye immediately, and my heart began to thud. *It couldn't be. Could it?* I hardly dared believe it.

'Is that you, Dad?' I asked it, under my breath, almost embarrassed in case the grass heard, and laughed at me.

I closed my eyes, waiting for a reply. *Was this it?* I'd know when I saw it, that's what everyone had said. They just knew. *Had he waited until now to show me where he was?*

If this was him, the buzzard would show me – something that only he and I would know. The secret nod. The comforting hug that he hasn't left me here, that he is nearby, watching us grow without him.

All I knew was that I needed this – I needed my sign. I waited for the feeling to come, the feeling that this was it. He was still with us, in some way.

I opened my eyes and searched the sky, but the buzzard had gone.

As we drove back to the safety of Ryans parents' house, we'd driven past Dad's house, and I'd braved a final glance.

Someone else's car was on the drive, and the bushes he'd planted out the front had grown tall and shaggy. His wooden blinds had been replaced with curtains, and the Green Man he'd hung by the window had disappeared. Then I saw something that caught my eye.

A banner on the door read – *Happy Birthday.*

Chapter 13 – A Jolly Story This Way Comes

As we meandered our way back down to the village, different memories kept flooding in. I was letting them in I suppose, enjoying the high and low of emotions I was rolling through, feeling like a little junkie for my own salty tears.

It was only as we reached the final stile, and the road split off into two – one way was the route back to the car, the other was down towards our old house. Dads house. I stopped still, staring down the road as a memory hit me, clear as day.

I have no idea why it had come to me now; I'd not thought about it for years – it had been stored away in my mental filing system, and yet – today – I felt I needed to revisit.

The story started with heartbreak – mine, obviously.

I'd been rather unpleasantly chucked by text.

This was before Ryan, although we'd already met and he'd stolen my heart. But as just friends, he'd been busy at college elsewhere, and I'd been enjoying the teenage need to be reckless and stupid.

My other best friend Matt had caught me mooning over old texts and dithering whether to text – The Dumper – in a half-hearted attempt to change their mind - or not - when he snatched my phone out of my hand, telling me '*This is how you get over someone!*' and deleting any and all trace of him from my phone. Including their number, so I didn't have the option to dither over it anymore.

He then wrapped me in a hug, pressed a Jack Daniels into my hand and told me 'Now what you need, is to get very, very drunk, with your best pal.'

So, we did.

At first, I was working – as a manager of a posh wine bar in town, but then when work started eating into our Getting Drunk time, the *audacity* of adulthood - I'd change the playlist from soft Spanish tapas music for the after-work-meeting crowd, to Nirvana around 9pm - to get the last of the middle-aged revellers to fuck off home. If this didn't work, I'd begin pouring half measures of whatever tipple they were drinking or collecting glasses from their tables. I'd sweep the bar – never next to them, as that would be rude – but just in their peripheral vision so they'd see I was cleaning up.

Finally, if none of those worked, I'd loiter. Wiping a table down next to them for a good six minutes. Then another. Whilst tapas music was designed to make time feel as though it was passing slowly – no lyrics, the same tune on repeat so you can't tell where the end of the song is. I'd then wipe the tables again - furiously fast and walk past them at a speed slightly quicker than usual. So, they'd feel the end of the night was coming sooner rather than later, which for them – it was. It was my first foray into anti-marketing, instead of 'getting them in', how to use guerilla psychology to 'get them out'.

My friends would then descend, and we'd gather a group of us for free shots at work, courtesy of my boss - without his knowledge - before clubbing into the early hours. Every night there was some sort of deal on, so we would hit the clubs in that order. £1 a drink on a Tuesday and Thursday, Free Entry there on a Friday, pub deals on a Wednesday and so on.

I hired my other best friend Jack, as my assistant manager, which was a recipe for disaster, and we ended up drinking the bar dry. We did what only eighteen-year-olds would think to do in such a crisis, and refilled the bottles with water until we could afford to replace them, gently distracting anyone from ordering from the water filled bottles and coaxing them into bottles of wine or champagne instead.

Thankfully, my boss was using the business as a front to money launder from his property developing, so he was pleased to see we were upselling the expensive stuff so brilliantly, until we woke up behind the bar one morning and realised that the jig was up. Jack banging on the front door with his wrist in a cast, and Matt the other side of the bar still snoring. I hurriedly quit before I was sacked, not waiting to hear the list of misdemeanours that had strangely - all at once come to light, with Jack following suit. A month later, the boards were up, and the business had disappeared. Whoopsie.

With a month's pay in my pocket and my heart still not fully healed, not working meant I was free to drink myself to oblivion even more often. Brilliant news. Mum and Dad had ceased to exist in my day-to-day, neither of them checking in to see what I was up to, so I began day drinking with my pub friends, Jack turning up with his dads Land Rover so we could pub crawl 'The Cotswolds Way' and falling in and out of fields and garden parties with my crew. When someone commented on how hard we were hitting the booze, I would retort - we were doing exactly what young people should do. And it was fantastic.

Then I met Oliver.

It was just another night; they'd all begun to merge into one. Chaos had ensued, and I had found myself friendless, in a dimly lit corner with an empty drink in my hand. I pushed through the crowds and headed to the bar to deposit the glass for a fresh, filled one.

As I made my way under flailing arms and around girls having their faces shouted into, a hand grabbed my arm and pulled me sideways. Stumbling out into the corridor, Matt began talking at a million miles per hour. Drunk, and probably buzzed off something else, he was telling me about some girls he had got chatting to and how he wanted me to talk him up to them outside. He pulled me outside to the smoking area and thrust a cigarette into my mouth.

Matt is the most confident guy I know, and women love him.

He absolutely does not need me to talk him up, although I love doing it because he is a sweetheart, and I love him. Yes, he's also an arrogant arse who knows everyone fancies him, but still – he has this vulnerability about him that means he needs his best pal to fall back on should they knock him down.

I do get it; he is a good-looking guy, and he has this way of making you feel like you are only person on the planet he wants to talk to. I fell head over heels when I first met him, back at college.

He moved classes in our second year, and we were quickly banned from sitting anywhere near each other.

Naturally, this had driven us even closer, and it was too late. I'd claimed him as my new best pal, and he had done the same. My crush on him soon dissipated as he became the friend I really needed. Besides, a guy can only burp in your face so much before the gleam wears off.

We seem to bring out this mischievous childish side in each other. He's got that cheekiness that makes you want to mother him, but also flirt outrageously with.

The other thing was - being Matts friend, you realise that he will flirt with anyone, man, woman or beast. There's no trying to be his type, as his type is anything that is keen.

And right now – his type are these two giggly brunette girls that he is hoping to audition at the same time to be the love of his life.

The audition doesn't take long, and before I know it, I'm holding his drink as he takes them back inside.

I smile at his back as he disappears, looking forward to the debrief about that tomorrow, as I know Matt will turn up, snacks in hand to ask me exactly where he went wrong with them?

Was it the toe-sucking? Or when he asked them to call him Big Daddy? I'm paraphrasing here, but you get the gist. Everyone loves Matt, myself included.

I smile to myself as I realise, I didn't get around to actually lighting my cigarette, and now my hands are full of one empty glass and one half-pint that I definitely won't be drinking. I look around for a table to put my drinks on, and fish around for a lighter.

'Need a light?'

I look up, and someone appears from the shadows, lighter in hand.

'Thanks,' I reach for it, but he flicks the flame for me and leans closer to light my cigarette.

I cringe thinking about it now, but I was jazzed up on alcohol, late teenage horniness and a desperate need to seem 'cool' about everything. Someone's head could have exploded out there, I'd have shrugged it off. I took a drag of my cigarette and leant against the table to smoke, trying to seem effortless, as though I don't need to make conversation - I read that in a magazine - confident people don't need to fill silences, as they never find silence awkward – and had immediately implemented it into my day-to-day behaviour. *Such is life.*

'You're welcome. Gylisa.'

My head snapped up at my name.

How on earth did he know my name? And knew it well enough to pronounce it right the first time. That never happens. Even my aunt still calls me *'Juhlissa'.*

'How do you know my name?' I ask him, trying to seem light and airy but all attempts at being cool and mysterious immediately dissipating.

'I've seen you around.' This mystery guy smirks at me. *Ahh, I see we read the same magazines...* I raise an eyebrow in response whilst I look him over. He was, quite obviously – a prick.

I'm about to ask, tragically, 'Where?' When Matt comes bursting through the double doors again, to the now almost empty smoking area, grabs me by the shoulders and starts yanking me back inside.

I pull back, telling him to wait a second.

'It can't wait, we've got to go NOW!' He is panicked and urgent, jumping up and down like a loon.

'I'll see you around, Gylisa.' The boy says my name again, hanging onto each syllable. He looks at Matt and I catch a strange smile creep over his face. It sends a shiver down my spine. I let Matt pull me away as I try to distinguish what that feeling was. It wasn't a good one.

Matt triumphantly shoves me onto the dancefloor for the starting chinks of 'our' song. We have made dance moves and everything. Almost every night Matt will hound the DJ into playing it, using a different and wildly untrue story each time.

'What happened to your ladies?' I yell over the music, as Matt starts flailing about and moshing to 'Call Me Maybe' by Carly Rae Jepson.

'They didn't want to share!?' He replies, indignant that they didn't want a rushed threesome in the toilets of this grotty place. I roll my eyes in response.

'How do you know Oliver?' He demands.

'Who the fuck is Oliver?' I scream back, as he knocks someone's drink into them whilst windmilling his arms around.

'That guy!' He shouts, trying to mop up the windmill victims now soaking trousers with his hands whilst still dancing around him. The guy is trying to fight him off, but Matt mistakes it for dancing, so embraces him, throwing him around like a ragdoll. His shouts are lost underneath the music. 'In the smoking area!'

Oh.

Oliver.

Where did he come from? How did he know who I was? I hadn't seen him before. Or maybe I just hadn't noticed, as I'm usually out with Matt who has a habit of-

'Shall we head off?!' It's Matt pulling me off the dancefloor as I am mid-arm swing and out of the path of the bouncer who has come to investigate how glass is smashed on the dancefloor, now making a beeline for Matt as the young lad, who has now escaped his clutches, and his friends point him out over the heads of everyone else.

We slip out the doors, and into the cold night air of the town.

Matt points me in the direction of the local kebbaby.

As we sit with two greasy trays of steaming meat and chips, Matt fills in the blanks in between bites of food.

'He's bad news, you don't want to get involved with that.'

'Why?'

'He's just not a nice guy, Gee. You could do better! You have only just been dumped by that arsehole – whatshisname…'

I don't know why, but it's suddenly irritating me that Matt thinks he knows better than me. Maybe it's a hangover from him deleting everything on my phone without asking.

Although he was right about that. Maybe it's because I hadn't even considered this mystery guy, and Matts assumption has irked me. Like I don't know myself as well as he does. My drunken mind tells me he's just jealous that his girls let him down and when he came back to find me, I'd found someone who did want my company. And then he'd dragged me away and basically got us kicked out.

He flicks a bit of kebab meat at me.

'You're not listening…'

'Matt, don't be a prick.'

'I'm not, I'm just telling you. No, sorry, I'm *advising* you. Find someone else.'

'I don't even fancy him! I'm not interested! We were just talking.'

'Oh great, well you can talk with someone else.'

He says it so arrogantly, so matter of fact, that he knows best, and that I can't be trusted that I see red.

'You aren't my DAD Matt; I'll talk to who I want to!'

'You just said -'

'I don't care what I said!' I huff. I get up and stomp off, kicking over my kebab tray and hoping some gravel and dirt has landed on his, leaving him to the mess, sitting on the floor on his own. It's a childish argument, fuelled by alcohol and immaturity but not like our usual scuffles.

Usually, it's Matt that gets himself into some hijinks and I berate him afterwards. *Oh.* The thought hangs in the air. Maybe I'm the one who likes feeling high and mighty as I advise him on the choices, he 'should' have made. *Huh.*

I don't like that thought so I push it down and tell myself I am right; Matt is just jealous that someone likes me, and he's been rejected. When he's come back to his safe bet, she was getting chatted up by someone else.

But now, Matt wasn't talking to me.

We'd spent the day hungover in my room, eating rubbish food and had sellotaped my phone to the wall so we had a screen to watch stupid YouTube videos on. It was the same thing we did every weekend. He'd brought the subject up about Oliver again and had earnestly told me he was just worried about me because he just didn't want to see me hurt.

I'd promised him I wasn't interested in Oliver at all, and explained the scene he'd stumbled into, and we'd left it at that.

Later that week we'd gone out again, Matt had gotten drunk and fallen onto a table of drinks, smashing the glasses and getting cut to bits in the process. As I'd been cleaning him up - Oliver had come over.

One or both had said something to the other whilst I was getting more tissue to mop Matt's arms up and punches had been thrown. As Matt had been pushed out the door by the bouncer from the week before, Oliver had taken my phone and called himself.

'Now I've got your number' he'd said, smirking at me. 'I'll call you.'

Matt caught the end of the conversation before being ejected and thrown a wobbler.

We'd ended up having a fight in the street, not a physical one – but both of us shouting at each other. Matt on his high horse, telling me he'd never pick someone I had warned him off, because he trusted my judgement and me shouting back that he never gave me the chance to, because he would ditch me for someone else at the drop of a hat.

We'd ended up in a taxi together and I'd tried to whisper to him from the back seat, but he wasn't having it. I stroked his arm through the gap in the seats, and he didn't push me off which I took as a good sign. But he'd slept on my bedroom floor and disappeared by the time I woke up in the morning.

 I'd text him but got no reply.

Two weeks later, Dad was washing up in the kitchen when a car pulled up to the front of the house. I spotted it out the landing window and went downstairs to investigate.

'Who's that?' Dad asks me.

'Dunno' I shrug.

It's a little sporty car, I don't know which. Silver. Not one of any of my friends own, and not one of Jacks either.

A text pings through.

'I'm outside. O x.'

'Ooo, who's Ox?' Dad asks, peering over my shoulder.

'None of your business!' I hide my phone and run back up the stairs, trying to see who is in the driver's seat. I could just make out a white T-shirt, and a crop of brown hair. Two tanned arms resting on the steering wheel. As the mystery driver leant forward and grinned at me, his pearly white teeth glinting in the sun, my heart sank.

It's Oliver.

How the fuck did he get my address? And why is he here?

Another text pings through.

'Knock knock.'

No, no, no, no. He can't knock on the door. I don't want him to see the house.

I look downstairs at the mess. Its dirty and cluttered. Junk fills every available space, Tom's computer taken apart on the dining table. I don't let anyone see the Hoarders Cave, unless I really trust them. Even then, sometimes.

My cheeks flare with embarrassment. It's already too much that he's outside. I can hear blood rushing in my ears as I try to push down that familiar feeling of embarrassment.

My school uniform always smelt of stale cannabis smoke.

It makes me cringe even now thinking about the chosen method my classmates would use trying to find their jumpers after P.E, everyone would lift their jumpers to sniff them, as they would recognise 'their house smell'. I would desperately try to find mine first, before anyone lifted it to their face and smelt the acrid smell of my 'home'.

Dad kept a pan of old cooking oil on the kitchen side – for later use, and cups were forever etched with black tea stains. I'd clean and hide a mug that only I would use, as the dirt would feel like it was under my skin otherwise, but Dad and Tom would use it, rendering it 'contaminated' in my obsessive-compulsive brain -

or worse – lick the rim and put it back to taunt me. I'd never know if it was really clean, or if they'd messed with it.

I'd spend hours cleaning one room to liveable status, but in a day or two it would be back to how it was. They'd call me a snob for wanting to live in a clean house, and Dad would make me a tea in the dirtiest mouldy cup he could find, only telling me he picked fur off it as I finished.

Food was often out of date or mouldy, with Dad chanting 'Waste not, want not!' or telling me how mould was good for me, as it was full of penicillin.

I'd chop back – 'We wouldn't need penicillin if the house didn't have its own eco-system!' but that was usually met with rolled eyes and 'Snobby cow!'.

I looked around at the kitchen, with drip marks of grease, mud marks up the walls, and a pile of crumbs swept 'neatly' next to the bin. Dads' half smoked joint in an ashtray on the side.

'I'm coming out.' I text back quickly, throwing on a hoodie and checking my hair in the mirror.

Dad calls me as I whizz out the door, but I ignore him, I'll worry about that later. I just need to get Oliver away from the house.

He's leaning against his car when I walk down the drive, my mind is elsewhere, worrying about my breath, what knickers I have on, how much *I definitely don't fancy him* and what he's doing here. Damn, I should have sprayed perfume, I must stink of the house. My heart thuds loudly in my chest.

'Hello babe.' He leers at me, and it makes me visibly cringe backward. He opens the car door for me, and I slip in, willing him to just drive us away from Dad's house, so I can relax again.

As the car door clicks shut, I notice the inside handle is missing.

It hits me then, the feeling I got when we first met.

The feeling that sinister smile he gave Matt as he led me away.

The creeping, heart thudding feeling as I recognised his face on the driveway.

Danger.

Chapter 14 – Danger

Olivers house, a huge architects dream, a world away from Dad's poky council hovel. It was like something from Grand Designs. It wasn't his of course, it was just him and his dad living there, I learned. His mum had disappeared not long after he was born.

He told me all of this whilst the tour was happening, until we ended up at the last bedroom on the top floor. His bedroom.

It looked just how I'd have imagined, if I'd cared enough to fantasise about him, which I hadn't. Large glass panels ran along the rear of the house, a patio sprawling across the expansive lawn. It was open-plan and contemporary but had a distinct emptiness to it. I took it in, making the right noises here and there, whilst trying to fathom exactly what it was that was missing.

As my eyes traced along the blank walls and empty shelves, I realised – there were no 'things'. Whilst Dads house was a hoarder's den of crap, books, artwork, records, ashtrays and miscellaneous. A lifetime collecting trinkets, our house was like a receipt of the life lived in it. This house was empty of anything but the essentials. No cozy blankets, no plants or flowers, no bric-a-brac or holiday souvenirs. No photos on the walls or drawers. No signs of life, at all.

He gave me grand show of his bed, raised on a small platform. His ensuite bathroom with waterfall shower. Everything looked as though it had never been used, apart from the wrinkle pillows and kicked off shoes by his bed. I didn't know what else to do, having not thought this far ahead, so played along. Oohing and Ahhing at everything as he pretended to humbly downplay it all.

He showed me the view from his bedroom window, and then turned to me waiting for a reaction.

'It's nice.' I said, lamely. Nice? I'd roll my eyes at myself if I could. He looked crestfallen, but only for a moment.

'I know what you need.' He countered, not registering my false smile and leading me up another set of stairs. I followed him through to a small office. He sat me down in the chair, which I idly swung to and fro. His back was to me now, as he fiddled with the combination to a large safe.

'This, might get you a bit more in the spirit…'

He opened the door and pulled out what seemed to be thousands of bank notes, a clear bag that held easily a kilo, or more of white powder. And something else… I tilted my head to make it out.

'A party!' He interrupted my gaze as he flattened out the notes and picked up the bag of powder, heavy in his hands. He looked at me for confirmation, but my eyes were stuck on the black handgun laid on the floor in front of me.

Was that real?

I wasn't sure what Olivers dad had done to afford such a sprawling house like this, and I wasn't sure if the gun was real either. The only thing I was sure - was my heartbeat filling my ears. Each thud spelled out the same word.

Danger. Danger. Danger.

He had already text his friends, many of whom I knew by name from the town. The popular crowd, gorgeous blonde girls and boys who lived at the gym. They descended, bringing with them a large dose of self-consciousness for me, and filling the front drive with their cars. A barbecue was wheeled out to the back patio. If I didn't feel so out of place, it would have been gorgeous. The sun was setting, casting everything into orange light.

The garden was huge – a football field, landscaped with trees and a pond at the bottom. In any other scenario I'd have pushed to walk around it, asking questions about the flowers and plants. Wanting to know what animals lurked in the water. Finding a hidden spot to lie on the grass, to listen to the birds, or watch for something magical to happen.

Instead, music blared through the sound system, in the house it was deafening, but the songs drifted out of the open doors and across the garden, lost out to the fields at the back. No one wanted to sit quietly in the beauty that surrounded them. They weren't purposely looking away - they simply hadn't noticed it in the first place.

Drinks were flowing and I found myself awkwardly perched on the edge of the patio furniture – not friendly enough with the girls to join in their conversation. Too nervous to speak to any of the boys, who were all gesticulating wildly about whatever sport talk they were into. Unsure if I wanted to find my place in this crowd anyway, but still lingering near to it, just in case.

One of the girls, Ellie, spotted me lurking and invited me to walk around the garden with her.

She was sweet, trying to get to know me and then using everything I'd told her to bring me into the conversation with the other girls. She asked for music suggestions, but they'd already played all the 'cool' music I knew, and I had no idea what else to offer. I shrugged lamely. I felt like a sore thumb, despite her best efforts. She tried to continue the conversation, so I told her I had an interview in a couple of days' time, and that I knew some of the girls here worked there already.

It was Matt who'd got me the interview, he said it'd be hilarious if we worked together. Just like college, he said. I was oversharing through nerves and alcohol, and I spilled when she asked me about Matt, blurting out that he wasn't talking to me right now. He didn't like Oliver.

'Oh, don't worry about that, he'll come round.' She reassured me. 'Ollies not so bad.'

She was sweet, and kind. But she was also not convincing. She led me back to the group and sat me next to her. I was in. Or so I thought.

I couldn't help but feel like I was being talked about.

The girls kept giving each other knowing smiles, and changing tact when I stared too long. It felt like school. I was interesting enough to gain the spotlight, but too weird to be accepted in. Instead kept at arm's length like a court jester, or a piece of shit.

That danger feeling was rising again. I told myself I was being paranoid. That I just needed to feign confidence and an air of not caring what they thought of me, and then I'd slip into this new social group. This first initiation would be a distant memory and one day it would be me whispering about some other poor new girl, self-consciously sat on the edge, waiting to be allowed in.

As dusk fell, Oliver led me into the kitchen, to introduce me to some of his closer friends, standing around the kitchen island. He hadn't spoken to me since everyone else had arrived, and I wondered if that had been a tact, or if he hadn't realised, I was his guest. As I got closer, I could see what they were hiding.

On a wooden chopping board was a pile of white powder, one boy was fiddling around with it, trying to create neat lines. The crowd opened to let us in, and all eyes fell on me.

Oliver handed me a straw, beckoning me forward. He made me do a little twirl, kissing my head as I looked on. I felt as though he was claiming me in front of his male counterparts. *Dibs.* The thought made me feel sick.

'Come on then, Party Girl. Show us what you're all about…'

I could hear my heartbeat in my ears again. The boys were all smirking and laughing, but the atmosphere had changed. I willed my face to remain polite, friendly. Innocent, even. Har har har, and all that. I painted a smile on that I hoped fooled them all.

We are all just playing silly buggers, aren't we. Olivers hand gripped my back and continued pushing me forward, and as I turned to look at him his expression gave me the sense of a knife wrapped in silk.

I willed my hands not to shake, as I accepted the short straw. To back out now would cause a riot, I'd be booed out of the house and wouldn't be able to show my face for weeks. This was the 'cool' group. Not my motley crew of wierdos. *This was my 'in'.* I leant forward and considered that I really didn't want an 'in' to these people. They really weren't my type. I could feel eyes on the back of my head. I could back out, you can always back out. Toe the line. *Say no.* Talk to fucking FRANK. Thoughts whirled in my head as I considered each action I could take. Wriggle out of it or accept the blow.

I closed my eyes and sniffed the first line of mystery powder without question. I bent down as though I were the Pin Up of Cocaine. I even raised a little finger as I held the straw.

The boys erupted into cheers and celebration, the straw was snatched away, and they each descended onto the drugs in front of us. My heartbeat felt faster than ever, as a cold, chemical drip fell down the back of my throat. I had no idea what that was. I wasn't sure I cared. My heartbeat felt like it was talking to me. Even quicker now. *Danger. Danger. Danger.*

The night slipped by as though it was on fast forward. Friends came and went; the girls had slipped off without saying goodbye. Just the stragglers left. It got light again, then dark. The drinks didn't stop.

Oliver had all but disappeared, and the faces at the house now were mainly male. I found myself outside, drinking a mixture of God knows what. How long had I been here? My phone had long since died, and I'd put it down somewhere and lost it. Even if I did call someone, I wasn't sure what to say. More drugs had been pushed on me, so when I looked at my reflection in the mirror, a wild-eyed crazy woman had been looking back. It had scared me so much I'd put sunglasses on to hide them. I couldn't ring my Mum, I felt too embarrassed. Dad wasn't an option either.

They'd given me a long lecture on drugs after finding a stash in my bedroom a few months before. Mum had marched me up to Dad's house to present the findings to him, before announcing they would flush them down the toilet. Dad had stepped in then, 'Er…let's not be too hasty with that shall we?'

They'd asked me what the contents on the tin had held, to which I'd lied as an attempt to convey some semblance of innocence. 'I don't know.' I'd shrugged, looking at neither of them.

Mum had hit the roof, telling me how silly it was to have accepted something if I didn't know what it was. She'd been trying to guide me and looked to Dad for back up on the matter.

Dad had been on his phone organising an impromptu gathering of his friends, to take place that evening. He'd 'confiscated' the drugs and told me he would 'dispose of them in a way he saw fit.'

Now I felt dirty and anxious. I would say I wasn't enjoying myself anymore, but I'm not sure I'd enjoyed myself at all yet.

I didn't want to be drunk anymore.

I didn't want to be high.

I just wanted to go home.

I had to find Oliver.

'Come here.' His gravelly voice meandered out of the darkness, again. Night had covered the garden once more; I'd not noticed when. He steps forward, holding a golf club.

'I've …um…been looking for you…' it comes out shakily. I don't even recognise my own voice now. It sounds as pathetic as I feel, and I berate myself for giving away a chink in my pretend armour.

'Well, now you've found me.' He kisses the top of my head as he breezes past. 'And I've found you.'

He's almost out the door when he stops to look at me.

'What is it?' He eyes me suspiciously.

'I was just wondering when you were going to take me home?' The moment those words leave my lips, I feel like a child for saying them. Shame colours my cheeks and Oliver looks down at me.

'I wasn't going to.'

He presses a golf club into my hand and walks back onto the patio. I'm at a loss at what to reply. Is he joking? I'm not sure. I'm not sure how to play this. I fiddle with the top of the club, pulling at the black tape at the top. He ignores my silence, before poking his head back through the doors to ask -

'Have you ever played golf?'

His tone throws me off, and in the absence of knowing what else to do, I decide to follow him.

'Not really. Well, crazy golf?'

He laughs in my face.

'That doesn't count…' I fill in for him, staring at the side of his face as he begins counting out paces and wobbling around the patio.

'It does not.' He agreed, steadying himself and dropping golf balls out of his pocket.

'I can play hockey?' I offer.

'Similar concept. Grab some cut grass off the lawn.'

I did as he asks, handing him a soggy wedge. Confused, I wondered where this was going. He placed the grass down in front of me, moves me into position, and places himself behind me. Arms against arms, hands over mine. He guides a swing back with the club and then releases my hands. I wasn't ready for the weight of the club in my hands alone, and stumble, nearly dropping it.

His hands find my waist, and he steadies me.

'Swing and hit the grass.' He instructs me.

I swing down with the club and the grass explodes into the air like a green firework.

'Excellent.' He muses. 'Again.' He drops more grass in front of me.

I look at him for explanation. He offers none. I swing, hitting the grass again, sending it over the patio.

He dropped a golf ball on top of the next wedge. Wordlessly, I hit the ball, it flies into the air and disappears into the darkness.

'Very good.' He compliments without looking at me. 'My turn.' He stands next to me and takes his own club out. His ball flies further into the abyss.

Hmm. I considered how to work this into my plan. I couldn't stop play and demand he take me home. At this moment, I think he might just ignore that altogether. I must play the game. Literally. Play to win. The prize is my freedom. My competitiveness comes into play. It's a welcome distraction. My next hit flies further still.

'OK. Game on.' Oliver's eyes meet mine and he smirks. I beam back. *Butterflies.*

Hang on.

No. I'm drunk. I'm probably still high. This guy is a wanker. He's spoilt and arrogant. His friends aren't much better. He's put me in a social situation I'm uncomfortable with. *Did I say I was?* No. *I accepted it.* His car is missing a handle. *Maybe it was just broken?* What if he is trying to manipulate me? *What for?* Matt said that-

Yeah, Matt said. Matt said he was horrible, and no one liked him. Matt said that he was 'bad news'. But his house is full of friends, or it was.

And Matts not here.

As my thoughts argue about whether my instincts are right or not, I swing again with the club, but it slips out of my hands and spins into a tree.

'Oh fuck!'

Oliver laughs, closes the distance between us, and kisses me.

Oh FUCK.

I pull away, staring at him for explanation. He doesn't offer one, but his eyes glint back at me. *Maybe he's trying to figure me out too.*

We continue with golf until the sun rises and starts to blind us. It's fun, he's not so bad on his own. Maybe that crowd isn't his either, I ponder. We chat about – well utter rubbish, probably – but it's easy. I make him laugh, and he surprises me with his view on things. I realise that for the last few hours I have been relaxed and enjoying myself. I look around at the mess surrounding us.

My first thought is that I'm sober. But I haven't stopped drinking, in fact Oliver has made sure I've had a drink in my hand at all times. We've cheered at great shots and drank for bad ones.

Oh my god, I realise. I've actually done it. I've drank myself sober.

Huh. *So that's what that is like.*

Oliver rummages in the kitchen, pulling out some left-over sausages.

'You need food.'

I think about it. I do not feel even slightly hungry even though I couldn't tell what I last ate.

I say so and look around for something else.

Everyone else has gone, I realise. The house is empty. When did that happen?

The kitchen is littered with bottles and cans, wrappers and half-eaten barbecue food.

'We should clean this up.' I say, as I start collecting packets and glasses, before realising I have no idea what to do with them. I arrange them neatly back on the worktop.

'Or... we can continue...' Oliver drawls from the walk-in fridge, throwing the unwanted sausages back in. 'Your phone is in here.'

My phone! I vaguely recall it getting too hot in the sunshine, and someone suggesting putting it in the fridge. I take it from him and try to turn it on. Nope. Dead. I push it into my back pocket, I'll find a charger later.

'What's the time?' I ask, looking around for a glass for some water. Thirst is suddenly burning my throat.

'Time - for some more drinks.' Oliver brushes past me, unscrewing a bottle of wine he's discovered in the fridge.

'Oh, I don't want to drink now.' I begin, the thought of more alcohol repulses me. Besides, I still need to get out of here. My head is throbbing, I must be so dehydrated. He interrupts my thought.

'Come on, Party Girl…I thought you loved a bender.'

He's not interested in stopping, even though it's well past time to. I wonder when he was planning on returning me home, kicking myself for not planning ahead. For throwing caution to the wind, as per usual. Now look. I'm still not sure if he was joking about taking me home or not, and now I'm not sure what to do. He can't drive me home like this, and I don't want anyone to see me in this mess. The bottles and cans, the white powder marks on every surface. Credit cards are coated in it. Spliff ends are dotting the floor. I haven't seen my reflection for a while, but I know it won't have gotten any better. My hair is matted and sweaty. My skin has lost its colour and looks mottled under the kitchen lights. My hands are shaky and weak. My mouth is so dry cactus would thrive there. Teeth so furry they feel like they're made of wool. I catch a glimpse of myself in the marble kitchen worktop and it confirms my fears. I look like a junkie.

'What do you mean?' I ask, trying to buy some more thinking time. How am I going to wriggle out of this. Whenever I've been in situations like this before, I've always had my friends with me. Hannah, or Matt. They always make sure I'm home safe, as

I do for them. It's easier to think when there's two of you. But Hannahs disappeared to Ireland, and Matt isn't talking to me.

I'm on my own.

'That's what I've heard. When I asked about you.' He continues, searching through the mess in front of us for something.

'She's always out. She's wild. *She's anyone's…*' He sneers out the last jibe, watching for my reaction.

What?

'That's not true!' I protest. It's not true, I wasn't that girl at all. I went out with my *friends*. We had a laugh and would come home again, all together. I was almost virginal at that point. Yes, I'd talk to boys and had kissed a few. Alright, a lot. But I wasn't. My cheeks burned. *How dare he suggest I-*

'Well, only if you have your 'boyfriends' permission…' He sidles up to me, jeering in my face. The penny drops, he wanted that to incense me. *He wants a reaction.* Everyone has gone home, so he needs a new game to play.

'I don't have a-'

'Matt this. Matt that. *Me and Matt are going to work together.* Me and Matt do this, me and Matt do that. My friend Matt doesn't like you. He said-' Oliver is mimicking my voice now, but a higher octave than usual. I hadn't told him about the interview, or that Matt and I wanted to work together. Ellie must have let it slip.

'Matt's my best friend!' I argue. My fists are clenched by my side. He's trying to bait me, I know it. But is he? Or does everyone think that? I'm not a cheap tart if that's what he's trying to insinuate. It feels petty to even get defensive over that. I know who I am. *But what if that's what everyone thinks?*

I want to argue, I want to tell him to stick his party, and his burnt posh sausages and his miscellaneous drugs up his arsehole. But I don't. *I don't fit in here; I don't fit in with these people.* I feel the need to defend myself, but I don't want to look stupid doing it. He'd go back and do impressions of me, my shaky high-pitched voice telling him not to call me a tart, or a slapper. That I'm here because he asked me to be. *Maybe I was what he thought – I'd hardly put a fight.*

Tears prickle at the corners of my eyes dangerously. Oh, how embarrassing. My mind fills in the gaps – Oliver laughing with his friends at my expense. *'And then she cried!'* All of them falling about themselves laughing at sad, pathetic Gylisa.

'You've obviously got feelings for him.' Oliver continues, brushing me away. He's found what he was looking for and begins to roll a spliff. I blink my tears away. 'But - if he's so special, then why isn't he talking to you? Got sick of you, I reckon.'

My mouth opens and closes at this cruel statement. There's so much to counter but my brain isn't working quick enough. He'd started out quite nice and fun, I'd begun to like him. Now suddenly he was the voice in my head. It felt like he'd manipulated enough information out of me to twist and use my worst thoughts about myself, against me.

'Come on...' He pushes past me, holding two drinks and a spliff as he heads back outside.

I feel so wrongfooted, but I don't know what else to do, so I follow him, feeling just as feeble as he wants me to.

He's sat on the patio, lighting his spliff. He throws a glass at me.

'Have a drink, you're so uptight.'

'I'm not uptight.' I say, coldly. I catch it just before it hits the ground, but don't make a move to drink anything. I still have my sunglasses on, which is just as well, as it's daylight again and the summer sun is blinding. Plus, my misty eyes would give me away, and I don't want him to needle at me anymore. I tilt my head to face the sun, hoping that Oliver sees that I simply don't care what he says or thinks about me. I'm confident-

'Come here,' He leans over and pulls me into a hug. It's not a friendly one, painfully crushing me against him, bending my shoulders tight. I've had enough but play along. My mind is whirring again as I need to figure out how to get out of here. *I need an escape plan.*

'Josh is coming over.' He's released me again and is typing furiously into his phone.

Josh.

I try to place a face to the name. As I struggle, the garden gate clangs, and he appears.

Ahh, Josh. Handsome Drug Lord Josh. Josh is a reoccurring character out in town – using his side hustle of dealing hard drugs to fund his party lifestyle through university. I'm not sure what he is studying, but it's something highbrow. Josh is the sort of boy you would take home to your parents for them to fawn over, completely oblivious that golf club he keeps in his boot isn't because he takes part in the game – it's for any regulars that try to take liberties.

He is the object of many of my girlfriends' fantasy crushes, myself included. He strides over the lawn and looks me up and down.

'Jesus, you look strung out.' He steps up to the patio and shakes hands with Oliver. 'Ollie.'

The pair of them walk inside, and I'm left on the patio, crushed.

Not for long. I formulate a plan. Josh isn't drunk and must have driven here. Maybe I can ask him to get me home. I feel desperate, sweaty and disgusting. No, I can't ask Josh. I don't know him. It's too embarrassing.

But it's the only viable option I have right now, so I force myself go with it. I just need to get to him before Oliver does.

My mind is racing as I make my way inside, I've got get out of this house. A small voice reminds me I've got an interview to get to, which seems ridiculous now, but my mind is shooting all over the place. It's like something mad is happening so I'm trying to escape to dreamland.

Silly things fling to the forefront of my mind, I'm assuming to protect me from the reality I'm in. A house with two men I don't know, one if not both of whom hold utter contempt for me. They aren't my friends. They are both much stronger, and scarier than me. My dream brain interrupts – I start fretting about not having any extra clothes with me. And I can't wear what I have on now. Oh god, I've lost both my socks. My feet are black on the soles from walking around outside for the last however many days. I fret about that too. Anything to keep my brain from finally understanding the magnitude of the situation I am really in. *Disassociation at all costs.*

I walk inside under the premise of finding a phone charger and my socks. I flit past the kitchen and see Josh downing half a bottle of whiskey.

Fuck.

I find a corner out of the way and take a moment to recalibrate. Maybe they'll forget I'm here and I can figure something else out. I debate having a shower, but I don't feel safe enough to get undressed in this house, so I stay put, arms firmly by my sides.

Drinking ensues, and Oliver catches me sitting outside, then tries to bully me into more drinking. I pretend to take sips and throw it onto the grass when he's not paying attention. Josh has brought more drugs around and keeps watching me suspiciously, wondering what I'm doing here when I claim I have a blocked nose, or wriggle out of taking part by making drinks or disappearing to the toilet. They are both lying on the patio off their faces, laughing and making fun of me whenever I appear.

Hours must pass, and I've been here for days now.

Oliver won't let me leave. I've gotten brave enough to mention it to him a few times, but he either shakes me off with a wave of his hand or talks gibberish back. He's hallucinating, and Josh has taken himself off somewhere to calm down.

Oliver is talking to someone who isn't there when I accept, finally, that Matt was right. I hate him for being right. And for not being here. I can't call him, my phones dead, and even if it wasn't – what would I say? I can't bear the thought of him gloating at me.

Oliver bursts into the living room and starts looking around wildly.

'Now what?' I'm bored of this now. I've tried playing along and exhaustion has finally hit me. When I breathe in my empty stomach growls back.

'There's someone trying to break in!' Oliver hisses at me, beckoning me over to him. I shuffle over to the nothing in the window. He grabs my face and points it at the empty window. I scan the area. Not even a blackbird. No signs of life at all.

'What?'

'Theres someone trying to break into the house. I just heard them!' Oliver presses his back to the wall then ducks beneath one of the front windows.

'It's the middle of the afternoon?' I reason with him, as much as you can to a strung-out posh boy who has overdosed on fuck knows what and has been wildly hallucinating for the last few hours. I start to walk over but he tackles me to the floor, with one hand over my mouth, the other pointing towards the empty back garden.

I look out the window to where he is pointing.

There's no one there.

'Holy shit! Did you see that?' He releases me from his grip and slides backwards towards the lounge. I look out at the empty driveway.

'No?' I trail off, bored of this new game he's invented.

I've had enough. Either he is trying to wind me up or he-

'It's a fucking tiger! Behind the bushes!' Oliver jumps up and shuts the curtains.

I have laughed but I don't think he is winding me up. His eyes are pure black and full of fear. He looks scared out of his wits.

'There's noth-'

Oliver pulls me to the floor again and shushes me, finger pressing painfully against my lips.

'Shut the fuck up. If anyone hears you...'

'Listen...' Realising that he is clearly suffering from some sort of drug induced psychosis, I whisper it to him. 'Why don't you check the doors are locked, and I'll keep looking out for someone. It might just be one of your neighbours checking in on you.'

I'm whispering in a calm, caring tone. I need him to hear me as the voice of reason. I make a show of looking out the window, so he knows I'm telling the truth.

'Oliver...' I turn back to talk to him. He's gone.

I see him skidding on his socks around to the kitchen. Fucks sake. I wait for a few moments, but he's gone into the garage. Presumably, to check it's locked so the wild tiger and/or crazed intruders don't get in.

Sighing, I throw myself onto the sofa, sitting arse first onto the TV remote. I pick it up and flick the televison on. Man vs Food booms out on the speakers underneath. I mute it, wanting to just use some visual stimulation to escape to. There's still music playing in the house somewhere, and too much noise is giving me serious mental overstimulation. Maybe this will just play out and he'll exhaust himself out, like a drug addled toddler.

I try to engross myself in the TV but the thought of anything to eat is repulsive to me despite my growing hunger pains. I try to think back to what I ate at the barbecue, but I think I was too nervous to eat in front of everyone, so I drank wine instead. That feels like eons ago now. I realise I don't even know what day it is.

Oliver sweeps up the stairs and out of sight again. I can hear him upstairs talking in low tones and try to block it out. The music playing on the speakers outside is filtering through so I can't quite catch what is being said. Maybe they'll fall asleep and then wake up normal. I hope so. Something else is digging into my arse, so I reach down and discover my long-lost phone. *Hallelujah.*

I try to turn it on. Texts and missed calls keep pinging through until it dies. I turn my attention back to the television and notice it's dark outside again. I feel like I'm in a strange dream. I watch the presenter gesticulating wildly when I notice the murmuring has stopped.

They've gone quiet.

They must have fallen asleep, I tell myself. But my nerves are on edge. My subconscious has picked up on something else, an invisible static that I can feel on the back of my neck.

My ears are straining so hard to listen for something that they start to ring. A soft creak behind me feels like a bolt of electricity. Was that my imagination, or was that real? I'm not sure at this point.

The living area leads out to the patio, with glass doors all around the back side of the house. I see a tiny shadow of movement out of the corner of my eye in the reflection on the glass. I freeze.

My instinct tells me not to move an inch.

The ringing in my ears gets louder. My heart feels like its frozen in my chest.

Danger.

Another creak of a floorboard, and I can see clear as day in the reflection behind me.

Danger.

Oliver has slipped back down the stairs, alone.

He is creeping slowly closer to the back of the sofa, to where I am sitting. Each step is slow, considered.

Danger.

I strain my eyes without moving single muscle to see what he is doing. I'm not sure I could move right now, even if I wanted to. I feel frozen in place. My eyes are screaming at me as I try desperately for watch for movement. My peripheral vision is going to be fucked after this.

Danger.

I can just make out an object in his hands, but the light in here is dim, so I can't quite see what it is. My fingertips feel like electricity is pulsing through them. *What has he got there?*

Danger.

My head feels static, as though all my hair should be raised on end. The hairs on the back of my neck feel like they could crackle. Adrenaline floods through my veins, icy fear replaced with hot fiery need of survival. I can hear my heartbeat start again, clanging away like a drum in my chest, but also slowly, as though time has stood still for a moment.

DANGER.

I hear his intake of breath as he slowly raises the object in his hands.

God, is this really it?

The air is almost hissing with tension as my mind flickers to my parents. Mum. Dad. *What would it do to them for me to go like this?* My brother, a twinless twin. My sister. Hannah, Ryan, Matt, the gang and everyone else I know, twisted with grief. What would it do to them? *How would they cope?*

My mind flashes forward and I see each of their faces, miserable and sad. My amazing, brilliant Mum - unable to let go, hoarding herself out of her boat, and onto the street. Dad, my strong, immovable force - lost to alcohol and grief turning into anger. My kind, fair brother, floating around lost and without purpose. My beautiful, caring sister, carrying the burden of grief for them all.

They wouldn't cope. They'd blame themselves. They'd crumble and waste their lives. Tragedy marring their life plans forever more.

All that mental self-funeral planning and I didn't think what it might do to the people I care about the most. It didn't even feel funny now to invite my adversaries to force them to listen to how great I am.

I was.

Was I? I counter that thought with another. I haven't done anything great yet.

I'm not done.

It screams over all the other voices in my mind, my brains last fight for survival.

This can't be it. Not yet. You haven't finished yet! There's more to come.

There must be.

I hear a final creak in the flooring, closer than ever and I dare not look at what is waiting behind me.

Oh God, what if I die here, and they might not even know.

No one knows where I am.

I didn't even say goodbye to Dad when I left.

I should say something, last words maybe? For the first time, I have nothing interesting to say. This might be the end, and I can't even think of one last wise crack to go out to. One last thing to be remembered for, even if no one hears it.

Oliver would hear it. I think bitterly, but I feel as though I can see into the future now - I can see him in my mind's eye, watch him walk up the stairs, splattered in my blood. Face distorted in horror as what he's just done wakes him up from whatever trance he's in. He walks into the office, picks up the handgun, and ends it all.

Blood finally painting some life into this soul-less space.

I close my eyes tightly, wait for the crack, the flash of blinding sharp pain, and darkness to envelope me.

Hang on.

Why have I given up already?

This isn't going to be it; all is not lost. That flickering flame of hope that has never let me down yet ignites again, with a point of a second to go.

It's telling me, no – *this isn't how it ends.*

Not today, pal.

My eyes open and dart around for anything in front of me that could be used as a weapon. *Fuck – a leather cushion – and the TV remote.* No good. I look at my hands, now balled into tiny fists. I could be quick, but I was certainly no match strength wise for Oliver. What did he have in his hands? A weapon. A gun? No, it looked like a bat, or a bar. A gun I'll never have a chance with, but a bat? My brain is calculating the options quickly, even my mind knows this is the last chance saloon.

I have to make the right decision, first time.

If I can just get some distance between us, I could have a chance.

A chance is enough, however slim. *It's not my time, not yet.* I must do something, at least go down fighting, if nothing else.

A condolence maybe, to everyone who knew me. She went, but with pride. She fought back. She tried her best. Getting my head caved in with no reaction? That's just not true to my character. People would start to question if they knew me at all.

It's time. My arm-hairs are on end, shooting straight up like cacti spines. I close my fists tighter and take a breath in. *I'm ready.*

Another creak, my spine tingles. I can hear his zip on his hoodie, the soft brush of his trousers as he moves in on his unsuspecting prey.

'What are you doing?'

Someone speaks, breaking the heavy tension in the room.

I realise it's me. My brain has taken over as survival mode kicked in. *Speak first, fight later.*

The next sound I hear isn't my brains being painted across the empty white walls, although - I think serenely - that would have certainly spiced them up a bit. It's the sound of wood hitting tile, as he drops the bat from his hands, and it clatters to the floor.

It *was* a bat, my brain confirms.

I spin round to look at him. Then the bat, to make sure.

Wouldn't want to have overreacted now, how embarrassing.

I repeat the question, adrenaline flooding my veins.

'I-I don't know...' His voice is shaky, as he walks around the sofa and throws himself down on it next to me.

Neither of us speak for a moment. My armpits prickle, my body trying to make sense of this new situation. My entire being isn't sure what to do with this turn of events, I'm still in Danger Mode. *How close had I just been to –?*

'I think things have gotten a bit out of hand...' Oliver's voice shakes out of him. Quiet, shameful.

'Have you calmed down now?' I ask, it comes out piercingly cold. I feel cold now, a shiver working its way through me - drenching the heat that had made its way up my spine. I'm going by instinct; I need to take charge.

Most of all - *I need to go home.*

'Yes.' He has his head in his hands, leaning forward. He must feel as lost as I do, and I'd almost feel sorry for him. But then he was about to redecorate using my brain matter, so I shelve that thought for now.

'I want to go home now Oliver.'

Chapter 15 - The Horrors Persist – But So Do I

Oliver still seemed shell-shocked, but I didn't want to miss my chance of escape, so when he leant down to open the car door for me, I flitted in. He was so wrung out and certainly not sober enough to drive, but I was willing to risk it for a chance at freedom.

'You said something about an interview – do you want to go? I can take you?'

'No, I don't.' I am exasperated by this question. I'm a mess; I've got no shoes on and want nothing more than to sink into a hot bath and wash away all memory of this event. 'I want to go home, Oliver.'

'I can take you home and then to the interview if you want?' He's pleading with me, the desperation on his face makes me feel ill.

'When will I next see you?' He doesn't wait for an answer, picking at his steering wheel and avoiding my gaze.

He must be joking, I thought. I never wanted to see him again. He was unhinged. Broken. Horrible. A Near Murderer.

'I don't know, I'll text you.' I don't want him to know I have no intention of ever speaking to him again - I'm too close to home, and too frightened he will turn around and take me straight back to the prison he calls 'Home'. I need to placate him, until I am in view of my house. We pull up outside Dad's house, and I try my best to smile and act the part.

He walks around to my side of the car and opens the door for me. *Aren't we a bit past the false chivalry now?* I wait patiently and don't thank him.

I begin walking up the driveway, holding my since-found socks and my dead phone, when I realise something isn't right. Perhaps it was a hangover, although I felt past that now. Perhaps it was a come down, although that must have passed too.

No, this was the dark cloud that had haunted me for most of my childhood, hanging over the house. Only I could see it, I knew that.

But I also knew that I needed Oliver to go home now. I'd only got in the car with him a few days ago to keep him away from this exact scenario. To keep him from seeing my life. I hadn't risked all of that just for him to burst into my reality now. He'd followed me up the driveway, trying to talk to me, to ease some comfort out of me from the last few days of horror. Why couldn't he just take the hint? I was getting dangerously close to just screaming in his face to 'Fuck Off'. At least then I could run inside and uncover whatever horrors were lurking in there by myself.

'What? What is it?' He was craning his neck, trying to see what I was staring at so intently.

'Nothing, just leave me alone-' I try to push him back, back to his car, away from me and my messy life. But he was crowding me, filling personal space, and tripping me up as I got to the back door. I'm about to elbow him out the way, when I try the door. It was locked, but Dad's car was there.

A deadly silence was cloaking the house, and a coppery taste was filling my mouth.

Something wasn't right.

Dad hadn't texted or called me, but my phone had died twelve hours into my disappearance, and I still wasn't sure how long I'd actually been gone for yet.

I walk round to the shed to find the key, Oliver still bleating on about God knows what, but I've blocked him out now, concern taking over my need to be polite to him any longer. I open the back door slowly and catch a glimpse of dried blood on the floor. Oliver steps forward and I move to block him out of seeing what I can.

'You need to go now, Oliver.'

'I just want to- what is that?'

He pushes past the door, stepping into my home without an invite, and staring open mouthed at the scene in front of us.

The house was cold as ice, and blood spatters littered the place. Down the stairs, up the walls, across the carpet.

The kitchen was the worst, with dried blood strewn across the radiator.

'You can go now, Oliver, it's fine.'

'Is that blood?' His voice was getting panicky, which was not what I needed right now. Getting panicked and stressed was the worst reaction to something like this. My nerves cooled instantly, my logical brain stepping into play. Something dreadful has happened yes but accept it and move on to the next – more important – thought. What has happened, and why.

Is there any danger? I doubted it, already formulating a theory as to what had happened.

'That's blood! Why are you being so calm?' His irritating voice was piercing through my thoughts, getting more agitated whilst I tried to piece together what had happened in here.

'Just go!' My voice was sharp. I needed him to fuck off now.

I didn't need this stupid rich boy, with his stupid rich life looking in at my trauma porn. Screaming and fainting over a little bit of blood, just because it happened to be where it shouldn't.

I had guessed vaguely what might have happened, and I knew that wherever Dad was in the house, he needed urgent medical attention. What I did not need was a jumped-up dickhead panicking and creating a scene for more people to gawp in at.

'You are so fucking weird; do you know that? Why are you acting so calm?!' Oliver was squawking at me. I pushed him back out the door mid-sentence, and that was when I saw Dad.

His body was in the living room, lying face down. I could see now that the blood splatters were a result of him flailing about helplessly in the house, until he had either knocked himself out, lost consciousness or was dead.

'Do you want to do something helpful, Oliver?' I shot back at him, trying to keep him from seeing Dad on the floor.

'Is that your dad?!' He was shrieking now. 'Is he-?!'

'I don't know, but what I do know, Oliver, is I need you to ring an ambulance. And stop being such a fucking baby about it. Can you do that Oliver?' I'm speaking to him like I would a five-year-old, trying to coax him into – not seeing sense as such, but allowing me to think for him.

He fiddled around in his pocket for his phone, face white and fingers trembling. He punched the number in and asked for an ambulance. 'I don't know your address!? What should I say?'

'Give it here.' I yanked the phone away from him and told the emergency line what I thought had happened, and where we were. I handed the phone back to Oliver and told him to wait outside for them, by his car.

Then I went back in the house.

The scene was of pure devastation. Dad had obviously made his way downstairs and tripped or fallen into the radiator and cut, what looked like, a large chunk of the back of his head off. Pieces of congealed blood, hair, and …well, lumpy bits were still stuck to the radiator. My stomach was turning at the sight of it.

He'd then stumbled into the living room, rolled around for a bit, judging from the pools of dried blood on the rugs, and lost consciousness.

I needed to see if he was a) breathing and b) still alive.

I knelt next to him and touched his skin. Warm. A good sign.

I studied his face, but he just looked asleep. A low groan came out of his nose.

He's alive.

I let out a sigh of relief, not realising I'd been holding my breath until then. I looked at the bloody mass at the back of his head. That, however, did not look great.

Unsure whether to roll him this way or that, I decided to not touch him, and to just let the paramedics do all of that. His chest rose and fell gently. Another good sign. See? I thought to myself smugly - *panicking will get you nowhere.*

I went back outside to send Oliver home.

'But your dad, and you. Are you gonna be alright? I can stay. If you want?' He mumbled the last part. I wasn't convinced.

'Just go home, Oliver.' He didn't need telling twice.

Sirens came into earshot, and I walked down to the end of the drive. They knew where they were going. This wasn't the first time. A police car followed. Behind that, my friend Jack. With another friend, Laura. In his mums convertible.

For Fucks sake.

The ambulance rushed in, and the police followed. Dad had form for being violent when he had one of his episodes, so they couldn't attend without a police officer being present. Which was ridiculous, and always enraged Dad – but this time he wasn't conscious, so I doubted he'd put up that much of a fight.

Jack pushed through the ambulance crews and walked up the drive to talk to me.

'What's happened Gee? We haven't heard from you for days and now there's all of this at your house. Are you OK?' Jack threw questions at me, but I didn't want to answer them.

His eyes weren't on my face but peering round to get a sight of who had been wheeled out there. I didn't respond, wondering if this was what shock felt like.

Tiredness had suddenly hit me, and all I wanted was to be left alone. And to have a bath.

The police officer began talking to me too, asking me for details and telling me they were going to take him in, asking me if I was OK and if I wanted to speak to someone.

'No, no..' I started, but I felt like I was dreaming now. I was waving my hands at everyone, go away. Go away. Everything felt fuzzy and far away, like I was underwater. Jack eyed me suspiciously.

'Did you do this? Gee? What's happened?' Laura joins him, having watched them cart Dad out on the stretcher.

'I just want to be left alone now, actually.' I answered them all waving my hands again to usher them away.

I wanted to close the door on the whole thing. I wanted to stop my two worlds colliding – my normal teenage world of friends, and booze and silliness and being young, was crashing into my real world – of Dad and mental illness, mess and dysfunction and needing to feel more grown up than I actually did.

I'd worked hard at school to maintain a safe distance between home and friends, and I worked harder still once my friends all started to 'drive round' unannounced. Who knows what they could turn up to, as quite often my house was World War Three. I closed my eyes tightly as I knew the questions that would follow. My friends meant well, but this was M25 Car Crash Gossip they would want to pick over for hours in the pub, without me.

The police officer guided Jack back to his car, which Jack complied with willingly as he had likely 'borrowed' it without his mum's knowledge.

'We'll call you.' He pressed on, face concerned and caring. But I didn't care. I just needed them to be gone. I needed them to disappear so I could assess the damage and begin the clean-up.

With that, they all vanished, Dad, the ambulance, the police, and my friends.

The house was empty again, the deathly silence now an endless void.

*

No one tells you this, but the emergency services don't stay to clean up.

They leave their gloves, and cotton and cut off clothing.

They leave you with the blood and hair and whatever else stuck to the radiator.

They come with noise and sirens and action, and they leave you with silence.

And you don't know what's going to happen next.

Is Dad going to die?

Will he come home again?

Did I do anything wrong?

They had confirmed what I'd first thought - that Dad had gone into a diabetic hypoglycaemic fit, fallen and injured himself. They weren't sure how long he'd been in a hypo, but it meant he'd flailed around and hurt himself more until his energy reserves had been so depleted, he'd fallen unconscious.

It wasn't the first time, and it wouldn't be the last. He'd survive with no memory of it, of course. It was always us that remembered. Always us that cleaned up. My sister had gone first, then Mum. Now it was just me and Tom left, and we'd had our fair share of cleaning up now too.

I filled up the sink with hot soapy water and began to scrub at the bits of scalp on the radiator.

The first time Dad had a hypo that I remember, was back when we lived in Yorkshire.

Mum had gone shopping with her sister, and I remember distinctly her saying to me and Tom…

'If Dad starts acting funny, just get him a Twix or something sugary.'

It had seemed like such an off-the-cuff comment, but for some reason, it had stuck in my mind.

A few hours later, Dad was at the computer, showing us something when he started slurring his words and talking nonsense. Tom and I had looked at each other, but Dad seemed otherwise normal, so we just laughed it off.

Then he stood up and started flailing about, picking Tom up and shouting 'Wheeeeeee!' as he threw Toms tiny 8-year-old body around like one of my dolls. The spare room had a mattress in it, thankfully, so Tom had just bounced off and flew out the room.

I went straight to the kitchen, but the chocolate cupboard was out of reach. I turned around to grab one of the dining chairs when Tom appeared, brushing himself off from his unexpected acrobatics.

'Dad's being weird, isn't he?' He giggled it out nervously, not wanting to be the one to address the giddy elephant in the room - one that looked suspiciously like our father.

'Yeah. Mum said to give him something sugary.' I didn't want to be the one to announce a potential emergency either. Finding an antidote to this mysterious illness was only thing I could think to do.

We set to work, making a syrup sandwich. Tom tried to make a sugary cup of tea to wash it down with as a back-up to our naïve plan.

We opened the door to the spare room, unsure what we'd find. Dad had fallen over on the mattress, kicking his legs about and gurgling like a baby. It was terrifying, not just seeing a grown man act like this. But our *dad* – go from being normal, relatively sensible and sane dad to a strange child-like man with eyes that wouldn't focus on anything.

It still felt like Dad was in there, desperately trying to get out, but a strange force had taken him over. He was battling with it, trying to fight whatever it was that had possessed him. We didn't have time to find it scary, or at least neither of us acknowledged our fear with one another. We just knew we should do *something*. Having Tom as my team-mate made me feel braver at least, I hoped he felt the same.

We tried to coax the sandwich in, whilst he swung his arms about and hit us, knocking us flying in turn, our tiny children's bodies no match against a grown man.

I realised we would need to try another tact and began speaking to him like a child. Or maybe I wanted to sound like the adult. Maybe I could get through to him a different way, I reasoned. 'Ooh try this, it's so yummy!' I tried to make my voice sound light and fun, pretending to eat it all myself.

He snatched it from me, crushing my fingers and the sandwich in the process, before flinging it around the room. As bread and syrup hit the window, I bit my lip as I inspected my fingers for damage. I didn't swear back then, being a kid, but I if I did, I would have said 'Bollocks.'

Thankfully, there were two of us, and Tom stepped in. 'I bet you are thirsty now, Dad?' Dad nodded wildly, and Tom offered him the lukewarm tea. He managed to drink some, before slopping the rest over himself.

'Oh, Noooo!' He wailed, upset with himself.

'That's OK Dad!' I encouraged him to take the remainder of the sandwich I'd salvaged from the carpet whilst Tom scrabbled around for the rest. 'Try this now, Mmm...'

His eyes glazed over and met mine, recognition flickering through for just a moment, before he nodded again slowly and began to eat it carefully, sugar from the tea finally proving to be the antidote to this strange madness.

None of us spoke for a moment, as we watched him chew in slow motion, before mumbling a lazy 'Tired…' and he threw himself backward onto the mattress again.

He fell asleep like that, sandwich still in his mouth, which worried me as I thought he might choke – but I wasn't really sure what to do about it. We waited in the hallway for Mum to return. No mobile phones then, so we couldn't call ahead and tell her what was going on. All we could do was wait.

She must have seen the black cloud over the house, one we all were trained in seeing without realising - as she rushed in and took control of the situation within minutes of arriving back. She kept telling us 'Well done for being so brave' and for remembering what she'd said. Mum was good like that; she always came to the rescue. Often late, yes – but she'd be there.

Since then, Dad had had numerous hypos, and 'funny turns.' You could never predict one, but I got used to the signs and could often catch them before they transcended into chaos, or danger.

Dad would get embarrassed as he heard what he'd done or said, so we stopped mentioning them, and he felt like we were patronising him if he was low on his blood sugar. You could tell as he'd start getting a faraway look in his eyes or saying things that didn't make sense. So, we would gently offer a biscuit as code for 'I think you are about to have a hypo.'

Often, Dad would have them in the morning, so we would wake up to him crashing about as his blood sugar had gotten too low overnight. It could be quite a shock to have to sort him out in the morning, sometimes he would have soiled himself too.

Then we'd race to get ready for school at the same time, worrying about whatever state we had to leave him in to catch the bus, often missing it. We'd get bollocked at school for playing truant, or bullied for looking untidy but I didn't want to tell anyone about what was really going on for fear they judge us, misunderstand or worse, take us away from Dad altogether. Plus, sometimes I just didn't want to be around everyone else pretending to be normal for the day, sometimes – I just wanted to hide in my room and wallow in the madness of it all.

I think back to all those times now, as I lay on Dad's bed.

The house is dark and empty, and I couldn't get the fucking blood out of the carpet, so I've left it all red and patchy and sopping wet. I slipped into the bath after that but couldn't relax fully. I felt like Dad's ghost was haunting the house and kept looking over my shoulder as I tried to shave my legs. I'd slipped with the razor and cut a slice out of my knee, given up and gotten out, leaving my hair dripping wet. My fingers had been scrubbed sore, and my stomach has finally started growling.

I would make a cup of tea, but I feel exhausted. Paralysed from the last few days events. None of it feels real, I think. My brain wants to take over and make me feel like I'm dreaming so that I just accept what's happened and move on to the next thing, not processing anything along the way. Like a dream, one minute you're deep in conversation with your cat, the next it hops on its skis and slides away. You don't think *'but my cat can't ski?'* you just think *'well that wasn't very polite.'* And continue your shop around backwards Tesco.

A shiver brings me back to this realm. Everything is just too overwhelming to process. I don't want to do it, but the aching cold of the house won't let me shut it out.

Car lights shine against the ceiling, and I sit up and groan.

Who's that now?

Ugh. I throw myself back onto the bed, hiding my face in my arms. I just can't deal with anyone else right now.

A car horn honks twice, and I go to the window. *Whoever it is, knows I'm here.* I peer down to the silver Volvo on the driveway. It's Jack. Still in his mum's car I see. Must have given the coppers the slip. There are two others with him, and I squint down to make them out.

He's still with Laura, who beams up at me, waving. And who's that in the back? I peer closer, but there's no mistaking the mop of black hair, or the glint of that nose piercing.

It's Matt.

They all grin up at me, waving their arms to beckon me down.

'Come down!' They yell. But I don't reply. I take a few steps back and throw myself back onto the bed. Debating. Two voices begin to argue in my head.

My two worlds have grazed each other.

I may need to face the music.

Your friends came back for you.

Do I want to see them though?

But they are here.

But they saw. They saw the mess. The chaos.

My reality.

They saw what I've been hiding.

My stomach knots with embarrassment. I feel as though I've been pushed on stage and had my clothes ripped away – it doesn't help that I'm still only in a threadbare towel. I can't pretend I didn't see their faces contorted with disgust, concern and disbelief.

I can't hide away now. I can't play pretend.

They saw it all.

And they came back anyway.

I lie there with my eyes closed for a minute longer, when I hear the unmistakeable sound of three people letting themselves in.

You fuckers. But I smile down into the blankets.

Jack enters the bedroom first, stuttering out that they didn't want to pry but they didn't want me to be alone, and then immediately changing the subject to what they'd been up to. It's a flurry of consciousness that Laura joins in, both their voices feeling like white noise. They ignore that I am face down on the bed, not responding.

Then Matt joins them. They both go quiet.

'What's gone on here then, ey?'

I sat up and looked at him, then shrugged. It was just so typical of Matt to cut through the tension with one sentence. There was too much to say, I didn't even know where to begin.

He knew that, so he was saying – *none of that matters if you don't want it to. We don't have to talk about it.*

I laid myself back face down on the bed in response.

Matt threw himself on top of me on the bed, crushing me flat and not moving. It wasn't a hug, as such. More of a planking situation. Laura burst out laughing and even the corners of Jacks mouth were rising. I could see them through the gaps in my stringy, wet hair.

'We knew you couldn't stay mad at each other for long.'

I giggled underneath Matts bulk and started to push him off. He threw himself to the floor and I made to throw a pillow at him, but he ducks for cover and yells -

'Don't! The Dad Slayer will strike again!'

A laugh is halfway out my mouth when I think - hang on, what?

'Is that what you- I didn't hurt my dad, *you freaks!*' I stop for a moment and consider what they'd seen. 'I-…' I trail off, unsure if I want to hear the answer, my eyes falling to the dusty skirting board instead of any of their faces.

'Well,' Jack began, 'We didn't really know what to think.' He starts fiddling with the hem of his jumper. 'We saw the police and ambulance and then you were there all cool and calm…' He waves his hand in the air in lieu of an answer.

'Then Jack asked the police-man-officer if you'd killed your dad, and they said they couldn't tell us what had happened.' Laura counters, shrugging her shoulders as though this was a perfectly reasonable explanation.

'So, they came and got me and told me you'd gone crazy and were on a murdering spree, so I asked if we could all go and see it.' Matt finished, getting himself off the floor.

'Then we figured, you were either murderous, or you just needed to see your friends.' Jack shrugged.

I look up at him, then Laura, before settling on Matt. They weren't looking at me in disgust, or concern, or disbelief. That was just what I thought they'd be. They didn't care about any of that, they just wanted to know I was OK. Jack gave me a small smile.

How lucky I was to have friends like these.

'Well, I'm not murderous, but thanks for the faith in me. And I do need to see my friends…' I laughed. They might be total idiots, but they were my idiots at least. And they cared about me. Or just wanted front row seats. Either way, I was glad.

'OK, but before we go, can we just check to see how murderous you are feeling? 'Cuz the last thing I told you to do was to Fuck Off, so I feel like I might rate pretty high on the Hit List.' Matt teased me, but he pulled me off the bed and to my feet. He leant down and asked me quietly, 'Do you want to talk about it? Or-'

Jack poked his head back in the door. 'Or do you fancy going for a joy ride in my mum's car?' He jangled the keys at me.

'I could do with some joy.' I shrugged back.

I raced to pull on some clothes whilst they waited in the car. Jack put the roof down, him and Laura in the front, and Matt and me in the back.

Jack flicked on the radio to 'Primal Scream – Loaded', he turned the volume up as high as it would go, Matt shrieked as loudly as he could, Lauras laughter echoed off the neighbours' houses, and I threw my arms in the air – and we disappeared into the night.

The silver linings were there really, I thought to myself as the wind whipped around us. I didn't know or care where we went. My hair felt like ice against the night air, and it tugged painfully on my scalp. I *was* lucky. I was *alive*.

Oliver was gone, as soon as he'd came. My friends closed around me once more and I heard word he'd left the county a few weeks later. Dad was going to be alright; I'd got to him in time. They'd have called if he was dead or dying. And if he *was* dead or dying, they'd call the housephone and leave a message – so that was tomorrow's problem.

For now, my friends were here.

They'd seen my secrets, and they hadn't run for the hills.

Well, not yet anyway. And that was enough for me.

I'd come as close to the edge as I'd ever known, my perspective unwittingly shifted, never to return to what it was before. I was alive. I was free. Everything after this point would be bonus.

I had to make it count.

Chapter 16 – A Life Worth Living

*Hello Ju, I'm sitting in the kitchen, it's Hale and Pace time on C4 Wednesday **December 2ⁿᵈ, 1992.***

We spent the day pushing the twins about town – well I did, but mainly to show off to everyone (even the guy who snarked on the corner of the street past the church)

You are all asleep! And I can hear people running about downstairs, I was just thinking about how I would provide the best chance or ability to provide or help or father for you, Clair, Tom and Gylisa. Even Jess, the old git.

You know what I'd like –(and this is an old dream) to have enough dosh for 1/3 of the lump sum, to go to charity, the other 2/3's to be split – one to buy a house or land enough to raise chickens, goat, pigs and veggies. The other to leave in an interest gathering place for them great bangs in life that need something to help you get back together. Like now, we've got £40 or so quid to buy food and no way of getting the food. I mean, I've been living on cereals for days.

Now what is this leading to? Well, Life is GOOD! But I yearn for the day it gets better!

As I know, or feel that it will, our lives will not always be squashed together like it is now. And maybe, just maybe a job will come along. Even extras...what a novelty.

Chapter 17 – Mirror, Mirror

Dad's diabetes really had been the unspoken taboo of our family life. Which was funny really, considering anything else was welcome. I wondered how he'd truly felt about it all, other than his admission to me so many years before. We'd been sorting through the airing cupboard in his room, when some heavy scrapbooks had fallen out onto the floor. I'd gathered them up and realised they were his, the scratchy handwriting recognisable even from his boyhood.

Dad had gathered them up, and explained he's been encouraged to make a scrapbook as a young lad. It had just happened to be the same time he had been diagnosed with diabetes – so he did what anyone with a diary does and shared what was going on in his life at the time.

He'd written about how strange it was to be diagnosed, although also a relief to know why he'd been having strange symptoms. Thirsty, all the time – nothing could quench it. Needing a wee constantly too, although he'd thought that was because he'd been drinking so much squash.

But most compelling, had been his child-like acknowledgement that something important had happened. He had been marked as different from the other kids. He'd not found the words to explain it, but he had intuitively known – nothing had really changed, but nothing would be the same again.

I feel a familiar pang of grief as I want to go back to that moment, sitting on Dad's bed and realising he was showing me something so private and personal. I wanted to say something more apt, more moving. To tell him how grateful I was that he'd chosen to share it with me, or how I hoped he could look back and reassure his child-self.

But I hadn't, I'd sensed that something poignant and important was happening and a strange shyness had crept over me. I'd flicked past those special pages and talked too fast to try and make the moment 'be over'. To try and make it less piteous and awkward. Maybe I'd picked up on Dad's emotion and felt I was prying. Like I'd sneaked a peek into his true self, the private thoughts that a daughter had no business looking at. And now, as an adult, I held another diary of his, and had devoured its contents without stopping, desperate to see into his inner thoughts, eager to find out more, to find answers to the endless questions he'd left us all with.

Another crushing realisation hits, and I sigh to myself. What's done, is done. Like looking at a home that has served its purpose, maybe it's time to close the door.

I busy myself then, back in Present Day – a time I have found myself living in less and less – I'm at home, back in Cornwall. In my haven. I begin cutting vegetables to start dinner. The ghosts of the past vanish around me, as I peel and slice carrots, muttering to myself just like Dad would in our kitchen.

I move methodically, finding the groove of autopilot that I've been reliant on the last few months. Clean the house, cook the dinners, organize the people. Do the motions, first it was an hour at a time, now it's days. The only thing that snaps me out of it is playing with Lily, but even then, it only takes a few moments before my eyes are misting up, and I'm wondering how Dad felt when we did this. I calculate the time he had with us as children, then as teenagers, then as adults.

It wasn't enough. Time is flying by, and I have only realised it now. I glaze over, holding an empty teacup I'm supposed to be sipping out of, or mid-conversation with one of her teddy bears, and before I know it – I'm so aware about needing to be present, and yet I can't bring myself to stay in the room with her.

A dark thought slips in, and I battle mum-guilt with the ache of grief again. It's a battle in my mind constantly, one I don't always win. I feel as though I'm the Eeyore of this household, bringing with me the cloud of depression in any room I enter.

What if Dad and I are more similar than I thought?

What if I leave my Lily like this, a broken half-person – wasting all of the *now* because she can't stop wishing for the *then*?

It's a cruel thought, and one that has dogged my evenings for more nights than I care to admit. I toss and turn at night, the right side of the bed constantly evading me, until I give up and let all those questions with no answers flood in.

Dad and I were so similar, but it feels as though it was in all the wrong ways. Everything I disliked about him – *stubborn, vicious, hot-headed.*

His self-doubt, but inflated ego.

His want of control driven by a lack of it.

What if I end up just like him?

Old. Alone. *No future.*

And how did he get there? It hadn't happened overnight. *Perhaps that was what scared me the most.* It had been an insipid drip, drip, drip into his life. Snapping at someone here. Demanding something there. We'd started so well, before Dad's invisible rules and mood-swings had taken over.

I think it bitterly, but what worries me the most – *I can see myself doing the same things.*

I realised early on that Dad's need for control was born from his diabetes having such control on him. Never able to be the carefree man he wanted, he had been forced to follow schedules, dietary needs and endless insulin injections at exact times. Every. Single. Day.

On my worst nights, I take solace in not being governed by something so out of my control.

Then the snaking fingers of guilt grip my feet and pull me in, as I realise – *I finally understand you Dad, and you aren't here to tell.*

Chapter 18 – Looking Back

25th April 1994.

We, or I and Julie, Clair, Tom and Gylisa have all moved into this house, Cheltenham. Big garden, veggies growing, job with parents (the only bummer). Money sometimes and the odd extra. Winks came back from Aussie land, going to university. Hans etc, all still pop round, although most have and are drifting away. Even Winks, which I hope is not long lived. Smurf and Max with son Harry pop round, and we have a smoke and do a little parenthood. But life is good(ish) and with Zen.

My only bum thought is I can't share what I have because those outside – don't listen. T.T.F.N.

Ps, I got a tent today for work, going camping in the back garden!

12 September 2000.

We have been living in this new house for two years now.

A tied cottage in North Yorkshire. Work has come, from study and work to make me a gardener. Tom and Gylisa are eight years old, Clair is 15.

We have through struggle and sheer determination become a family of good human beings.

May 30th 2008.

Back in Gloucestershire, living in Mickleton. After lots of hassle, including being diagnosed with depression in 2004 following bankruptcy. Julie has left me and the kids. Clair is living in Cheltenham with her daughter. Julie and I have fallen out after many months of hassle, she has decided to leave for good.

This I am not so much happy about as relieved, as I now have control over what happens in this house. Tom and Gylisa have just left school hoping to go to college. I am working in Hailes, recreating a lost garden. Still poor.

Although earning £21,000 per year, life is still very expensive, and I am sort of lost with no real direction. I've lost Zen and art and realised I have been stoned for far too many years.

Monday 11 November 2011

Mickleton: At the end of this year I'll have been living in this village for 10 years. Everyone has grown and left. Julie lives on a barge with boyfriend. Clair is in Evesham with two daughters. Gylisa is living in Cornwall with boyfriend. Tom is still at home but at 21 his time to move on is now. Re-reading this notebook again, it has been a fab life. All the friends and fun times.

I'm 47, self-employed and with new vigor for life. Recently changed my insulin and quantity. This happened after an incident of hypo for three days. Anyway, I survived and have lost weight and now I can eat less. Parsley went blind.

With some meditation and life experience I have a much calmer personality, sadly it's taken me the majority of this life to find a nice person.

This note is a little random but I have lots to say and few pages to get it in...

A few months ago I was at Smurfs when he confessed that I was his closest/best friend. I mention this only because he and I met at the age of 6, waiting to go to 'thickie reading classes' and over the years have had our differences. (I haven't forgotten E.T.)

But he has spent a whole load of time meditating and we have both matured and become the people we wanted. But poorer. Music is a great way to feel love.

I miss the family, and although I don't regret anything, I do regret not enjoying the time with the family AT the time. To not enjoy I mean too busy, too stoned, too tired, too grumpy. It's all gone now.

With all lives my part in their lives was small but I hope great enough that approach to life and passing on my love did have an effect.

Anyway, I'm alone – yet have many visitors each week, so happy that I still listen to music, play games and toke with my friends.

W I C T J I L H.

26th Feb 2015

Hi. Am still sitting in the kitchen, it's 9am, a Thursday.

I work for myself, and the council have decided to insulate the house.

Everyone has left, grown up, etc. Clair has 2 daughters and another on the way.

Gylisa is expecting her first.

Tom is off to city living.

I have struggled over the last few years with my health, diabetes and mental problems.

I am hoping the eviction notice the council have put on me will not be enforced. It has come about because I haven't paid the rent properly.

I work occasionally as a self-employed gardener. This is a rambling note, as have wanted to write but have been unable to see a task and then complete it.

It is fabulous that the sprogs have grown and as young adults are making their lives…

I am alone.

2 Dec 2016.

Fuck! I'm 50!

Although still think and feel like I'm 16. I have had a good time, if you look across the 50 years there has been no end of hassle but mostly I have smiled everyday.

I'm a grandad. Four granddaughters.

Nov 21 2017.

Tom has just visited. He interviewed me on his podcast…

The night before on a usual session with us, for the first time I went to bed first. It was glorious moment that will help him become the gentleman that is in him.

We shook hands at the passing of the throne.

Chapter 19 – Autumn

The leaves are beginning to turn.

The next season is creeping in, first one tree – then another – I'd been watching it from the view out the living room window. Morning mists had been settling down the valley, and I'd found myself no longer rushing the school run, to get back for the release of my cherished Grief Hour but taking the scenic route home. I'd spotted a herd of deer by the woods one morning, and had begun a routine sneak around there to see if I could catch them again.

I didn't always see them, but instead started noticing things that I'd been too insular to notice a few months before. Cobwebs with the clinging morning dew. Crows migrating out of the woods for the day. Even the hares didn't run when they saw me now, instead ambling a few feet away as I walked through their route. I'd become a regular morning fixture for them, as they had for me.

With Autumn rolling in, my dental appointments had finally come to an end – my teeth were straighter and whiter than they had ever been. It had been a bizarre change for me – I'd spent so many months being miserable that I'd hardly noticed when the smiles had started coming easily, and I no longer reached up to cover my mouth when they did.

Laughter had begun to creep back into the house, although it had never been too far away – now it came easily, it wasn't followed up with choking sobs, or wistful glazing over.

Autumn meant the looming reminder of November. One Year since Dad had left us. I tried not to focus on it, and instead got busy with friends, dinners, wife-work and being Mum.

Cornwall is at its best in Autumn, the sun is still shining, but the beaches are now empty – it's when we explore the most, great stretches of sandy beaches without another soul to interrupt.

Ryan decided to take us to Fowey one Sunday afternoon for lunch, and as we explored the shops and walked off our meal, we rounded the corner to an unexpected crowd by the quayside.

A man walking against the tide of strangers caught my eye. I recognised him. The familiar dark mop of messy hair, weatherbeaten tan from the summer sun. Checked shirt and filthy jeans.

Dad?

As soon as I see him, he's lost again and my eyes search through the heads all moving against me. I feel as though I've been drenched in icy water. 'Dad?' My voice says it for me – that was him, I'd recognise him anywhere.

'Dad!?' I call it out now, dropping down into the crowd and pushing through trying to get another glimpse of him. I couldn't believe it – *it couldn't be?* But hope thrummed through my body as I started elbowing people out of my way. It's September for Christ's sake, where have all these people come from? I felt as though I was in a dream, everyone seemed to be heading the opposite direction to me, and I kept losing my footing on the uneven ground. But I had to get closer, I had to see him. All the while my mind was having an argument with itself.

It was Dad. *It can't be.* But I saw him. *It's not possible.*

What if it was all a ruse? What if he just wanted some peace and quiet? What if he faked it? *What if, what if, what if?*

In my haste to get ahead, I realise I've lost Ryan and Lily. I look back to where I'd left them, but I'm lost in a sea of faces. The tide of the crowd pulling me further away from where they stood. *They'll find me,* I thought to myself as I ducked down to push past a family who had decided to take up the whole pavement. I bobbed back up to try and find that familiar crop of hair, or the gait that only Dad has - but I couldn't see him.

I stop still, and someone behind me knocks into me sharply.

'Watch where you're bloody going!' The stranger hisses as he moves around me. I don't react, I'm still scanning the mob for Dad.

He was here. Had he'd seen me? I search for his familiar checkered shirt, or his always-dirty-jeans. My contact lenses start to fog as I refuse to blink in case I miss him.

A hand touches my elbow, and I spin round. *Dad?*

I search the familiar face in front of me, but it's not him. Ryan offers me a sad smile and shakes his head. 'I thought it was him too for a minute…'

He pulls me into a hug, arms heavy against the disappointment that chokes me. 'I really thought it was him…' My voice is broken, I don't know if I'm saying it to him or to myself.

Ryan doesn't need to say anything. It wasn't him. Dad's hair had been fully grey when I last saw him, I remember now. He'd not had dark hair for a while before that either. He'd been skinny and fragmented. *I'd been looking for the wrong memory.* Even if Dad wasn't dead, I'd have been mistaken.

If hope alone could have brought him back, he'd have been standing in front of me a while ago.

But it can't.

It can't.

Chapter 20 – Acceptance

15 June 2018 –

Hi! Have given up gardening. It was that was a short meal made.

Now 22 June 2018.

Yes, I wish to give up gardening. (Longer conflab.) My fantastic son put himself out there and came to visit me. What a great human. The other two are also fucking great. That hug at the train station was outstanding.

Thankyou.

Totes Love You All.

That was his final entry.

A few months later he'd gone.

Never to return.

I'm sitting with Dad's diary open on my lap, staring at the words until I can blink and still see them under my eyelids. I'd been waiting for this day to come, naively hoping that the moment the time ticked over – to mark One Year since he'd gone – I'd be cured of my grieving, and ready to just 'get on with things'.

Instead, I'd found myself counting the hours until Lily's bedtime, so I could sit with a cup of tea, several Kit-Kats and cry into Dad's diary until he materialised in front of me and said 'Sike! I was just having a year-long joke with you all!'

Ryan had offered to sit with me and talk it over for the three hundredth and sixty-sixth time, but I'd declined. I'd thought about going for a walk, but it was misty and cold outside – and I wasn't sure where I'd go anyway. Dad had never been here, so it's not like I could sit on a bench and talk to his ghost.

Now I'd pored through his diary, I'd learnt so much more about the man, I'd sat with his private thoughts and feelings and re-read his life as he'd known it.

When Dad had died, there had been a big question mark around the nature of his death. As I sat with the warmth of the log burner wrapping around my legs once more, I closed my eyes and took myself back, back to this fateful week one year ago.

I need to go back to the night Dad died.

On the 3rd November 2018, Dad had been at Grandma's house– where he had ended up living following the eviction from our family home in Mickleton.

He'd then got his keys, made an excuse as to where he was going and headed out. He'd driven half-way to Stow, when he pulled over.

On the front seat of his car, was a photo of me and my brother.

He'd not taken his insulin and had fallen into a hypoglycaemic coma. With the lack of insulin, and being in the cold, it had not been looking good.

He'd been found the next morning by a dog-walker, unresponsive.

An ambulance had been called, and he was whisked away to Gloucester Hospital.

Five days later, in intensive care – he took his last breath, and shuffled off this mortal coil.

I drag myself through the mishmash of facts I'd been told. I remember rushing to ring my mother, when I'd seen my sister update her social media once he'd reached the hospital. I berate myself for having to be told to go and visit him, as I'd been so confused as to why everyone was being so serious.

Had I? Or had I known exactly what Mum was trying to say?

Had I known as Hannah cancelled her plans to take me to the hospital to see him that night?

Had I known as we walked up to the quiet ward, and the nurse had spoken to us in hushed tones?

I think I had.

I think my brain had just wanted to protect me from the impending hurt, so it had told me half-truths, to keep me in the safety of denial.

This happened to Dad, a lot.

It was just another mishap. *It was just another accident.*

He'll come home and get a telling off from his doctor.

Mismanagement of Diabetes.

That's what the coroner had said.

It had meant that Tom and I received his pension, and that he'd been released for the funeral much faster. It was a pre-existing condition. It was a risk for people with diabetes.

What were you doing out there, Dad?

Did you think it would be easier if we didn't know for sure?

Dad had diabetes from the age of seven. He knew how to manage it. He knew he'd paid into a pension for just over a year and half. He knew that suicide might mean we wouldn't receive it without a battle. It had been his final gift.

The still image of him, slumped forward in his car in the dark went through me like a knife. I longed to have been there, for someone to have been there. To have found him quickly. For this last year to just be a nightmare we could wake up from. So, we could make amends. We could know what we stood to lose.

Instead, I sit with his diary and great sobs fall out of me again.

Dad had gone.

Each sob brought a wave of that sobering reality.

I'd been holding out on remembering his final moments, of really examining each decision that had led him to the end – that I'd not considered that it simply didn't matter.

Dad had died, but there was so much of him left around me.

Dad might have gone there on purpose, or he might not have.

It hadn't been a decision or a conclusion for anyone but him to make.

Reading his diary, he'd had a life worth living – I'd been so hung up on him needing to keep living it, I hadn't considered that he might have felt finished.

As he had shed the last of his ties to the world – his home, his work, his belongings - even the cat. He'd been faced with all the remnants of a life that had been well lived. And as it occurred to him that the sun was setting in his life, it had just begun to rise in ours. We'd been so busy living our lives that we almost hadn't noticed that Dad had decided to start packing up for the day.

As he looked at his remaining parent, and saw her health starting to fail, her mind going with it. I wonder if he considered that could be his fate next?

I close my eyes again, lying back into the sofa and letting every thought crash in, tears keeping a slow but steady flow down my face. Perhaps instead of feeling like a burden now, as I'd assumed he'd felt when we'd tried to rally around him during the eviction – he'd sensed that he would be a burden in the future.

Better to duck out now, than be unable to in a few years. A true Irish goodbye, only this one was forever.

Why waste his time saying his last piece, when we'd all have argued for him to stay. All learning nothing, and just forcing him to long out the night because we don't want it to spoil our day.

He had bailed, before it got weird and awkward – before our memory of him was tainted with anything else. Now I thought about it, I realised he'd said his goodbyes months ago. We just hadn't realised. He'd gotten round to us all and spent one final day. The last photo I ever took of him was as he pushed Lily on the roundabout – one that years previous he'd broken some kids arm on. He'd gotten a bit carried away with the fun and had spun and spun until some dopey kid had fallen off. Whoopsie. We'd all known better, and having been on the receiving end of one of Dad's roundabout pushes – you clung on until it stopped. No breaks, no intermission. *And you enjoyed it!*

A smile works it's way on to my face, but I keep my eyes closed tight.

Perhaps in those last months, he'd been trying to push us away to save us from the pain of grief that he knew would come for us. *How wrong he'd been.*

After a year of reading through his diary, I finally feel as though I understand the man. I'd learnt his worries and triumphs, his opinions and aspersions. I'd followed his journey to be who he was to me – a father. That feeling, for once, isn't followed by the usual pinch of grief, of longing for him to be here for me to tell him.

Instead of wishing for him to be here, I wish I had been with him – in those last moments. Someone holding his hand, telling him it was OK. *I understood.*

For the first time, I realise he's been with me this entire time, I'd just not known how to tune into it.

I'd spent a winters afternoon in the rain, this time last year, furiously digging the hard earth to plant daffodil bulbs, just the way he'd shown me. Crying and muttering to myself. Telling myself that it would give me something to look forward to in the spring.

As I'd dug, and my fingers had first turned pink, then numb with cold – I'd noticed the sleeping signs of the trees around me. The winter flowering shrubs, and the branches soon to bud again. I'd realised that I could see life even in the dead of winter. Dad had taught me all of that, without me even noticing. Even now, as I pushed each bulb into its bed, I realised that I'd only known to plant now because Dad had taught me so.

Even in his absence, things would still be able to grow.

The following Spring, the daffodils had burst into life, turning the grey, forgotten garden into a cacophony of yellow and orange and white. I'd marvelled at them. I'd been hoping they'd feel like a gift from Dad, but instead they'd been a gift from me, to me.

Perhaps then, I'd realised that to conquer this heavy grief, the answers would be within me – not in him, or his diary.

That only by putting the hard work in, during the cold, would I enjoy the fruits of my labour when the warmth came again.

And now, here I was. Still standing.

Still a bit tearful, yes.

Battered and bruised, maybe.

Do I feel strong? No.

But I feel ready to be strong again.

I felt finally ready to accept - Dad had gone.

No matter how many times I'd asked him back. No matter how many wishes I'd wasted on it. He wasn't going to come back to save me.

I'd have to do that myself.

I opened my eyes and realised I'd done it.

Acceptance.

The final hurdle.

Chapter 21 – The Final Curtain

The most peculiar thing about grief is that it doesn't really go away. I didn't wake up cured after reliving his life until the end. After finally understanding that he was dead and accepting that as fact.

A bit of an anticlimax after all that, especially if you were hoping to get through this and learn 'The Secret to Conquering Grief.'

There is no secret.

I began this book by telling you that grief will happen to you, and it will. Grief will take your parents, and your friends, and your family members. It'll snatch them away and *it'll always, always be too soon.*

But I also made a promise that you would get through it, just like I did. I'm not a guru, or particularly special or wiser than anyone else. I'm just another person trying to make my way through life, one day – grief will snatch me away too. But if I can get through those first dreadful months, then you can too.

Five years have passed now, since I lost Dad.

Five long, full years.

So much has happened that he has missed. Sometimes, that feels unfair. Sometimes, I think he'd be bloody glad.

My grief has morphed into something much more bearable, or rather – I have morphed around it. Occasionally, I'll think of something he'd have done or said, and I feel that familiar breath-catching lump return to my throat as I achingly remember he is no longer here. I feel as though I've gone to reach out to touch him before remembering there's just empty space there now.

More often though, I feel him rush past me in the wind, or twinkle down in the stars. I hear him in my voice when I have to bollock Lily for something, or sense him in my fingers when I create something beautiful. I hear him in songs he loved, I smell him in woodsmoke, and I argue with him in my mind over my parenting decisions.

I don't really, of course, not the tangible way I'd feel if he was actually stood next to me. I just want to say that, to save you the disappointment I felt when I kept looking for him, wanting to receive the special sign that everyone else said they had when their loved one passed away.

I'd considered him selfish for not remaining with us as a ghost, watching us live our own lives, wither and die– how could he not want that? What sort of Dad was he?

I'm still not sure what I believe in terms of The Afterlife. But I know this much, if Dad had been offered the choice of watching us float around miserably, unable to touch or communicate with us properly - *or* - offered the chance to step into the next, exciting and unknown realm – he'd have jumped through that portal without a second thought. No chance to hear the 'Terms and Conditions', just 'Send me through!'

That's the sort of man he was. A dreamer, a vagabond and an adventurer.

I'm comforted by that thought, the same way I would be if he were simply 'abroad' or busy driving somewhere with no signal. Instead of desperately needing to reach him, to feel his presence or needing to know where exactly he is, I can simply let him go with the comforting thought that he isn't gone,

He's just on to the next adventure.

Final word –

You'll be pleased to know that I design my own funeral considerably less these days. I do occasionally argue with someone and dream out a slideshow of all my best bits to taunt them with upon my sudden and tragic demise, but on the whole – I much prefer to live in the now.

I suppose that sort of thinking is natural now that I've felt the unforgiving bite of grief on my arse, but I also think it's because I have my daughter to think about. I have no plans of going anytime soon, until I've taught her all she needs to know, and I feel she is well equipped to cope with whatever life wants to throw at her. Of course, I also know that I may not get the choice to hang on for as long as possible, although I do make a point of checking once, twice maybe even a third time when crossing the road these days. You can just never be too careful.

As I read Dad's diary, it struck me how similar we were, and I spoke to my Mum about this recently. (You'll be pleased to know that the family did all get back together, and not long after Dad's passing – Grandma joined him. Her funeral had been expected to be a stiff, sombre affair – but I think all of us had become so exposed to death and dying by that point that we ended up having a great time, a true celebration of life. How it should be, really. No fighting, no arguments – in fact, I had such a great time when I returned home, I kept mistakenly referring to it as 'Grandma's Wedding.')

I explained to my Mum that I was worried I'd make the same mistakes, and one day – I might leave Lily with no proper goodbye, no friends and no family around me.

Mum had told me, in her sagest of voices, that Dad had made his choices, and not once had it been too late to unpick any of them. He'd been aware of who he was and continued down his own path. Maybe out of stubbornness, maybe just out of fear.

The difference between us was vast – I hadn't just inherited Dad's genes, I had also gained her kindness, clarity and love. I'd added the sunshine, optimism and introspection on my own.

I didn't have to follow in his footsteps in misplaced honour. I was able to sing his praises and point out his failures in the same breath. I can do the same to myself, I think it's a worthwhile quality.

I didn't want to make a Saint out of Dad, because he wasn't one. He was a grumpy, miserable bastard. But he was also brilliantly funny, kind and interesting. I loved him, so I grieved him. It's as simple as that, really.

When it comes to my time, I'd like to think that I'll be ready to go, but there's no guarantees. Maybe I'll be clinging on, trying to get a few last seconds in before grief comes for everyone I love, or maybe I'll greet it gladly, knowing that they'll get through it eventually.

I'll be wanting to see what the next adventure holds…

The End.*

*for now…

Acknowledgements –

To **Dad** – I wrote you in the first book as a true bastard, and that's 'cuz you were. But you were also amazing, interesting, funny and silly too. And God, you loved us. But we loved you too. There was an entry of your diary, and it was this – *2017 – When I have died, give this diary to the Irving Welsh Diary Project.* Well, I did one better Dad – I published it. Your words are out there now, for anyone to read. Hope you don't mind! Too fucking late now, ey? Oh, and I cracked your code, and I told her. She knew anyway. And I do too. Thank you for everything Dad, even the shit bits. I'm a proper belter now because of 'em.

To **Mum** – my darling Mummy. Thank God you are still here. Don't expect a book when you go, they are fucking hard to write, and if I was to publish one of your diaries it would take me centuries! Then I'd have to pass it on to Lily, and then her kids if she has any – and so on – a generational curse I could live without. Thank you for being there, thank you for loving me. I love you too, so much. I may not have chosen you as parents (thanks Tom!) but I was blessed with you instead. Thank you also for filling in the gaps and answering my endless questions. Thank you for being honest, and for curling up that dead cat. I love you.

To **Hannah** – My best friend, my other soul mate. You have been through the wars by my side each time. When I look for you, you are always there, how truly blessed I am. Please can I peg it first, because I'd be lost without you. I'm not sure what we wrote in our blood pact, but I'd like to make an amendment to the T's and C's now.

To **Ryan** – Thank you for being my rock when Dad carked it. And all the other times. Thank you for never ever moaning about me snail-trailing your jumpers, and often appearing with a cup of tea or an ear to whinge to. Thank you for being my husband, and for being Lily's Dad. You are OK sometimes also. Love you.

To **Matt** – whom I fondly call Cat Poo, but didn't write that in, as I couldn't be arsed to explain it, and felt was mean to write in this bit as I knew you'd want recognition, you arrogant arse. You have been a shining light for me so often, you brilliant human. We really lived a lifetime together. I miss you deeply. Love you!

To **Tom** – I doubt you'll ever read this, but if you do manage to get this far, thank you. Thankyou for being Mr Sweden, and for always being the voice of reason. Even when you called that lady a bitch. She *was* a bitch. To my other family members, if you read this to him without him reading the book, you owe me a grand. Each.

To **Clair** – Yes, you can have an acknowledgement. I love you too. Please don't take offence to my recollection of things, you are a force of nature. You are brilliant, and beautiful and I am glad to have you as my sister. If I had someone else, I'd sack them off and come find you. Don't read Toms bit to him, I'll know it was you.

To **Dads friends** – You brought us up too, and I hold you all responsible for my disgusting sense of humour now. You are all stand-in dads, and brothers and friends. Hans, Geza, Beanie, Blob, Bomber, Spike, Shaggy, and Max, Lisa, Alice, and gorgeous Sarah. I love you all, beyond words.

To **my fantastic followers** – Thankyou for believing in me, for following my silliness, my sadness and more. I can't remember life without you, the cheerleaders that live in my pocket. How you found me I don't know, but I am grateful every single day for each and every one of you. I read everything you send me, I check every comment. And I love you all. Thankyou, for making my dreams come true.

To **Bhuna** – my black, furry, four legged co-writer. You are snoring as I write this. I told you you'd get a mention.

To ***my darling, wonderful Bear*** – It doesn't feel right leaving you off, even though we haven't reached our years yet. There's so much more to tell, and so much more to come. How lucky I am to have you in my life, in our lives. We have our pact, but should the worst happen – and I shuffle off before you. I hope you find comfort, wisdom and love hidden within these pages. I love you very much. Thank you for everything you do.

And finally – to **you**, wherever you may fit in my story – whether I know you personally, or I don't. Maybe you are already grieving, and someone has recommended this book to you. If so, I am sorry for your loss, and hope you too, find something in here for you. Whether that's the path to acceptance, for them or for you. Maybe you aren't grieving yet and this didn't make any fucking sense whatsoever – blame the editor! No, don't. One day you may return to it, and realise it all fits in.

Whatever your story is, this was mine.

The calm after the storm.

After laughter.

Printed in Great Britain
by Amazon

48375652R00118